VO

Musings of a Southern Lawyer:

A Collection of Commentary and Observations from the New South

J. Wesley Casteen, Esq., CPA

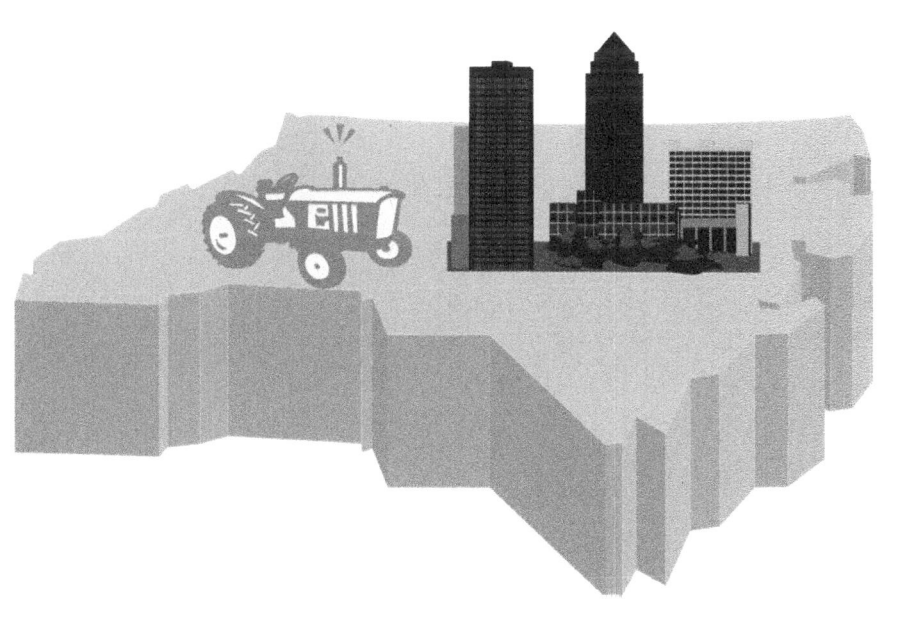

COVER ART FROM FIRST EDITION

© 2012 by J. Wesley Casteen

Second Edition - 2014

ISBN-13: 978-0-9914912-3-0
ISBN-10: 0991491238

All rights reserved. No part of this book may be reprinted or reproduced without prior permission in writing from the author or publisher.

Printed in the United States of America.

Publisher:

The Art of Word Publishing
Post Office Box 12028
Wilmington, North Carolina 28405
Telephone (910) 509-7209

Contact the author: wesley@casteen.org

For more information: www.casteen.org

NOTICE TO THE READER

No copyright is claimed in the illustrations or artwork contained herein. All such artwork and other works not original to the author are believed to be in the public domain, or the use of such materials is believed to be consistent with fair use as provided by law.

The information contained herein was believed to be accurate as of the date of original publication. Subsequent events or changes in laws may affect the accuracy of some time-senstitive information. Portions of these materials have been edited or revised from original publication in order to reflect such changes; however, efforts have been made to remain true to and consistent with the original work.

This publication is designed to provide general and educational information in regard to the subject matters covered. The publication of these materials should not be construed as the rendering of legal, accounting, or other professional services. If legal advice or other expert assistance is required, the services of a competent professional should be sought.

Any US tax advice contained in this publication is not intended to be and cannot be used for the purpose of avoiding penalties under the Internal Revenue Code (IRC) or under applicable state and local laws, or for promoting, marketing, or recommending to another party any transaction or theory addressed in this communication. This notice is provided pursuant to rules and regulations imposed by the IRS to ensure compliance by attorneys and CPA's with requirements under Circular 230.

Unless otherwise indicated, all original works contained herein are subject to copyright by J. Wesley Casteen, Esq., CPA.

Also available: Volume II

MUSINGS OF A SOUTHERN LAWYER
VOLUME II

J. WESLEY CASTEEN, ESQ., CPA

In Paperback and Kindle Versions

www.amazon.com

TABLE OF CONTENTS

PREFACE 1
SOCIAL COMMENTARY 5
   The Broken Social Contract 7
      Introduction - 7
      Social Contact as the Source of Government Authority - 8
      The Untenable *Status Quo* - 9
      The Expanding Roles of Government - 11
      The Master Becomes the Ward - 11
      The Breach of the Social Contract - 13
      The Evolution of the Social Contract - 15
      Society as a Collection of "social contracts" - 16
      Coordinating the Social Contract with Collective "social contracts" - 19
      To Whom Much is Given ... *Some* is Required - 20
      Enforcement of the Social Contract - 22
      The Whole is Greater than the Sum of Its Parts - 24
   Generation "X" Gets Thrust into Middle Age........................27
   Truth as Media Road Kill..33
GOVERNMENT AND POLITICS 37
   Healthcare Reform: It's as Easy as 39
      Where are we now?..39
      What does it mean to be "Uninsured"?................................40
      How did we move from Personal Choice to a Moral Imperative? 43
      What do we learn from experience? 44
      Is Trillion the new Billion?...47
      Who will foot the bill? 49
      What happened to Self-reliance? 50

Where do we go from here?..52
Tyranny of the *Status Quo:*
"Defense of Marriage" in North Carolina 55
Tyranny of the *Status Quo* – Speech Text..............................63
Oxymorons and the Republican Party......................................71
Occupy Wall Street ... the Leftist Tea Party............................75
Why watch Jerry Springer when you have CSPAN?.............76
Founding Fathers Turning in their Graves 77
"Never take a hostage you're not prepared to shoot."............79
TAXATION..81
A Rose ... I mean LOOPHOLE ... by any other Name 83
"Let's give the Government a little extra this year." - 86
A Rich Man Moves to Town..88
BUSINESS AND COMMERCE 89
"Welcome to McDonald's® ... May I help you?" 91
Someone has to do the "Dirty Jobs" – Titan Cement.............93
"Old" Does Not Mean "Historic"..95
Beach Renourishment..97
Big Cranes, Bigger Deal..99
RELIGION AND PHILOSOPHY 101
The Bible and the Ten Exceptions 103
Individual versus Institutional Morality 109
Righteous by Whose Definition? 111
Is there really any such thing as a "Nonsectarian Prayer"?...113
How [NOT] to Win Friends and Influence People................115
On knowing Light through Darkness 117
On Morality and the Law 119
LAWS AND CRIMES 121
There Should Be a Law . . . Really?.......................................123
The Immigration Debate 129

The Scarlet Letter: "F" 133
MISCELLANEOUS 143
Happiness versus the Pursuit Thereof 145
"The Ten Cannots" by the Rev. William Boetcker (1916) ...147
Melvin v. Easley, 7 Jones (NC) 356, 52 NC 356, (1860) 148
ABOUT THE AUTHOR: 150

This Second Edition is dedicated to the many family and friends, who encouraged me to run and supported Casteen for Congress. Thank you!

PREFACE

I have no notable talents in the arts beyond appreciation. Any avocation that I have arises from my fascination in the power derived from the spoken and written word. I do not mean the power of poetic verse, which may cause one to emote over some aspect of life or our surroundings. Instead, I make reference to the prose of philosophy and reason. It is the ability of words to convey the contents of men's hearts, souls, minds, and characters that I find most fascinating.

By reading and listening carefully to the sincerely expressed words of others, we come to understand those things that are important to the writer or speaker. We are allowed a glimpse into the processes of their minds.

My talents and skills, such as they are, come from education and learning. I was first trained as a Certified Public Accountant ("CPA"). Today, I practice as an attorney-at-law in southeastern North Carolina and my vocation continues to involve issues related to business, finance, and taxation.

I have been fortunate to have had the opportunity to learn from noted academics and scholars. I have learned also from students and colleagues from points all over the country and globe. Most importantly, I have been afforded the privilege of living in this great state of North Carolina and learning from its people, who are my family, friends, and neighbors. Each of these experiences is a part of the tapestry that makes me who I am today.

Over the last several years, I have shared some of my thoughts on issues that I believed were of general interest to others in the community. My thoughts and words were shared in articles, letters, and commentary. The audience was at times limited and at other times quite broad.

Some of the writings were intended to be more scholarly and included significant research and analysis. Other pieces, like the blogs entries contained herein, may have arisen off the cuff in response to a particular question or event. Still other pieces have been culled from series of online discussions or communications with friends and colleagues.

It is my hope that these articles and essays convey sincere thought and reason; although, emotion and personal opinion can never be completely removed from the equation. I do not write to impose any commandment or to offer any special enlightenment. It is only through discussion and debate that we can glean truth and understanding. That is my goal: A better understanding of people, life, and myself.

As you read some or all that follows, I am certain that there are parts with which you will not agree. It is not my objective to convert anyone to a particular way of thinking. I would prefer that each person reaches his own conclusions based upon his own careful reflection, thought, and contemplation.

Consider the essays an invitation to start a dialogue. I have provided the opening lines. From those opening lines, you have a better understanding of how I would approach the subject or address the issue. However, definitive "yes" or "no" answers are rarely included in the writings. If the questions were that easily answered, no discussion or debate would be required.

I am certain that I have a great deal more to learn, and I look forward to the discussions and experiences that will confirm my observations or provide a better insight and perspective on developing truths.

"Debate ...is not the celebration of common thought. It is the purification and forging of ideas through the smelting fires of discourse."

— J. Wesley Casteen, Esq., CPA

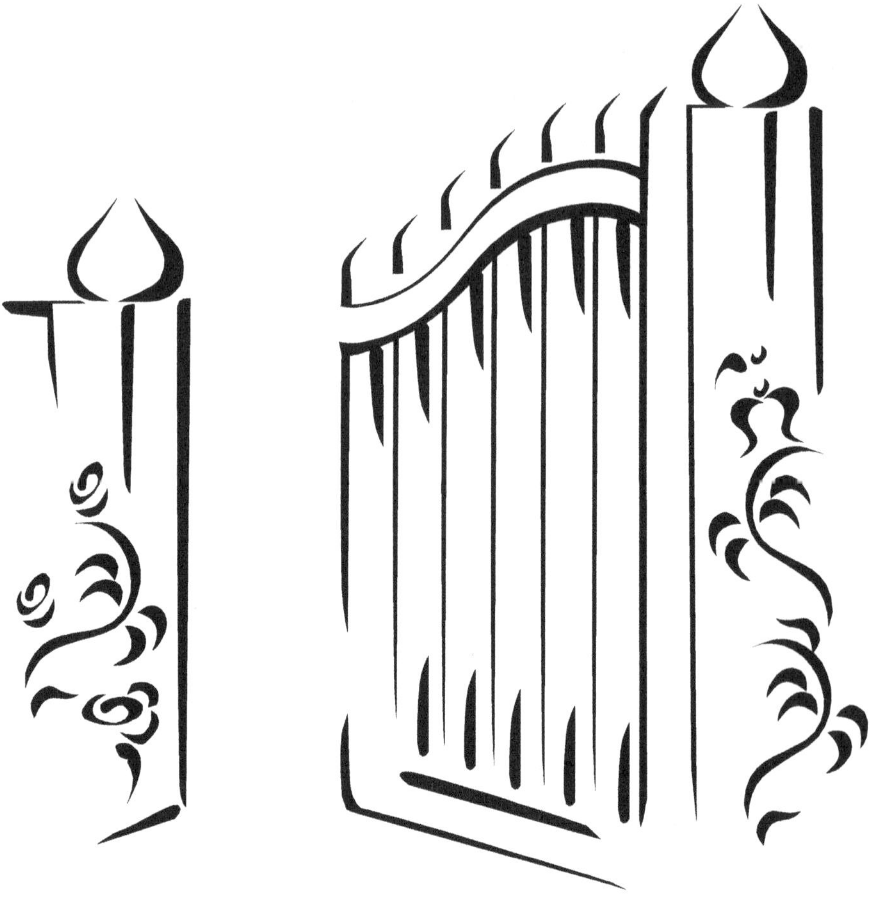

I.

SOCIAL COMMENTARY

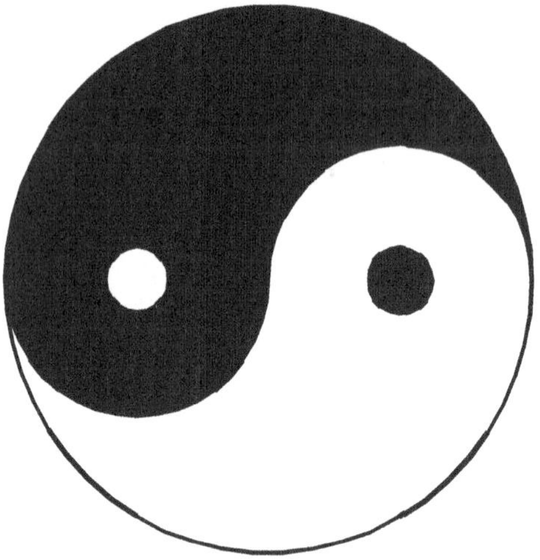

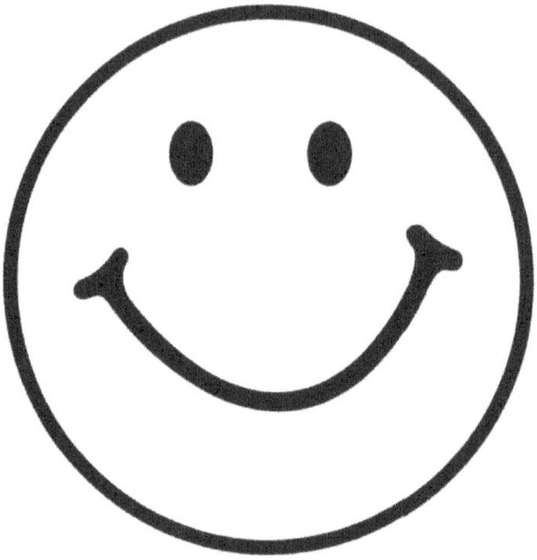

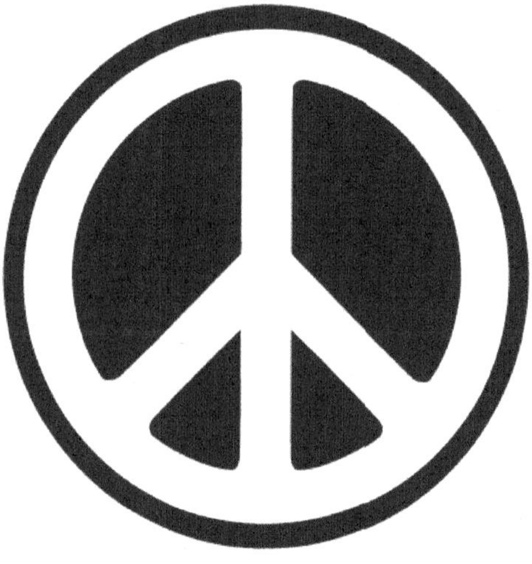

The Broken Social Contract

J. Wesley Casteen, Esq., CPA – © 2011

Introduction -

We have all heard the adage, "To a man whose only tool is a hammer, every problem looks like a nail." From this adage, we should learn that not every problem can be solved in the same way. Similarly, we must accept that one size usually does NOT fit all. These concepts are particularly poignant in considering the ever changing roles of government.

In law school, it was always interesting how professors from different disciplines would approach the same issues or facts in trying to arrive at a resolution to a problem. Many times the end result was the same, but the applied methodology often varied depending on whether the favored discipline was: Torts, Property Law, Criminal Law, or Contracts. Being an attorney and CPA, my point of view on many issues is often colored by the economics of supply and demand and the relationships defined by the law of Contracts.

Consciously or not, each of us engages daily in series of seldom acknowledged and unspoken "social contracts." These contacts may be personal as between ourselves and our coworkers, family members, friends, or neighbors. Or, the contracts may be collective as among groups and classes of people, or between the government and the governed. This latter relationship is the foundation of the formal "Social Contract" theories upon which the notion of "government by consent of the governed" is based. Nevertheless, social contracts exist in nearly every aspect our lives.

Legal contracts have several required elements, and these elements are often common to social contracts:

- An Offer made (essentially an invitation to contract or agree);
- Acceptance of the Offer (another party agrees to the terms being proposed);
- Consideration (*quid pro quo* – One thing in return for another); and
- Legal Subject Matter (consider in relation to limitations on the powers of Government).

Social Contact as the Source of Government Authority -

Under established theories of Social Contract, persons give up certain rights and freedoms in order to exist in the relative safety and to enjoy the protections and benefits afforded by Government. The individual submits to the collective will of the governed, and the Government enforces the tenants of the Social Contract for the benefit of the collective.

In the United States of America ("USA"), the powers of the Government are limited so as not to infringe unnecessarily on the individuals' natural or inalienable rights, including "life, liberty, and the pursuit of happiness." In return for the protections, comfort, and certainty provided by Government oversight, we surrender the right to act with impunity in all things. Few of us ever consciously entered into this contract, but it exists nonetheless.

In the USA, the Government does not have unlimited power, which is normally vested in a sovereign authority. Debates about the proper role of Government represent continuing attempts to interpret, define, or apply the Social Contract that gives power and authority to the Government. Recently, political debate has become polarized, and the language used is often expressed in hyperbolic and absolute terms.

We forget that the Social Contract is subject to amendment, revision, and renegotiation. Instead of reasoned discussion, certain privileges and benefits have been placed off limits by couching the debate in terms of inalterable rights and entitlements. However, few who demand access to those rights and entitlements have acknowledged any obligation to sacrifice or contribute in order to assure availability of the same or to impair any personal act in return for the government protections.

The Untenable *Status Quo* -

The existing debate is predicated on the notion that proponents are always right and the opponents are always wrong. Similarly, popular thought contends that for every problem there is a single and immediately discernible right answer. It is unreasonable to consider every law as a vested right, and we should not invoke the powers of the Government to promote our every whim or defend against each perceived injustice. Social problems are the results of years of action and inaction by numerous parties, including lawmakers and the citizens that they serve. Such problems are not cured and corrected by fiat. We must accept incremental successes and also incremental failures on the parts of our politicians. While we should not reward failure, we should accept changes of course as inevitable parts of the process. The true failure lies in not trying or in creating obstacles to productive growth. When we expect perfection and cannot accept sincere effort rather than guaranteed results, we are guaranteed timid and ineffective leadership.

With every additional involvement (some would say intrusion) of government, there are inevitably opposing groups asserting disparate "rights," which are being infringed upon by each government action. Civil discourse, which is a necessary cornerstone of efficient and effective government, has all but disappeared. Sincere energetic debate, with the objective of divining a refined truth, has been replaced with rhetoric, lies, and innuendo (from all sides). Negotiation has turned into stalemate.

The rub comes when my pursuit of happiness is perceived to be impeded by your desire to exercise certain liberties. It has been said that, "The right to swing your fist ends at another's nose." Today, the more aggressive of us wants to know with scientific certainty to the nearest nanometer how close that swing may come without resulting, not just in chastisement and rebuke, but also in significant personal cost and consequence. The more timid amongst us wants not only to be free from the physical assault but also to avoid the perceived threat of such an assault occurring at any point in the future. To say the least, these objectives are difficult, if not impossible, to reconcile to the satisfaction of all persons.

The Expanding Roles of Government -

Historically, disputes and disagreements were personal and handled man-to-man. In the case of the USA generally and the federal government specifically, Government provided a forum of last resort. The availability of such a forum is a necessary element of civilized society. In order to forestall anarchy, those with grievances much be given a forum in which to have those grievances heard and resolved. As a civil society, we require mechanisms for establishing laws, enforcing laws, and entering judgment upon those who break those laws. Nearly no one would question the need to punish thieves, rapists, and murderers. However, the role of government has changed. The rules which are promulgated today involve the most intimate and detailed aspects of our lives. Increasingly, persons question the propriety of the "price" of such protections or of the reasons for extending government into such areas. The issues focus on whether the application of the Social Contract under the circumstances is "legal" given the restrictions placed on our Government.

The Master Becomes the Ward -

Extensions of the powers of governments have created agencies and bureaucracies that act *in loco parentis* (in place of parents) over all of the governed, and governments have worked to establish systems of laws, taxation and benefits covering all aspects of our lives from cradle to grave.

The highest joy that any parent can have is to see a child succeed independent of the parent. No offspring can reach his or her full potential sheltered in the nest or home provided by the parent. Eventually, most children will choose to leave the nest eager to establish their own identities and to become self-sufficient and autonomous. Others may have to be nudged from the nest, but a disservice is done by the overly protective parent. Except in extreme cases, we must trust that persons have the abilities and tools necessary to assure their own well being, and that these persons will act in their own best interests. Where that trust proves misplaced the shortcomings should serve as a cautionary tale to others not a reason to deprive the opportunity to the many that prosper.

What does it say when government, acting *in loco parentis*, never sees the governed as being capable of taking care of themselves? What incentives do we citizens have to assume responsibility for our individual lives if the public dole is seen as the primary source of security? What disincentive exists to those that would seek to use their skills and labors to succeed when the government imposes impediments to that success in the name of uniformity and an ill-defined notion equality of outcome (as opposed to opportunity)?

The Breach of the Social Contract -

Unfortunately, many persons do not realize that they are a party to the Social Contract, which gives rise to these relationships. Ignorant of the nature of these relationships, many people do not participate in the "negotiations" that lead up to the established agreement. In establishing Government, the contract is negotiated through civil debate and voting. Where persons do not recognize or accept the binding nature of the "contract," they run afoul of the established rules resulting in personal harm or collective inefficiencies. Oftentimes, persons want the benefit of the contract without the obligations, but one cannot be had without the other.

It is often forgotten that part of the Social Contract requires that we abide by the established laws of the Government, even when we do not personally agree with them or when arguably they are not in the best interests of us as individuals. Yes, all of us recognize the need and power of occasional Civil Disobedience in order to effect change where bad laws are entrenched and protected by a recalcitrant government. However, simply disagreeing with a law is not a license to flagrantly disobey it, and if one does disobey such law, he must be willing to suffer the consequences of that action, even if done in the name of Civil Disobedience.

In recent years, even our federal government, led by the Justice Department and Presidents, have publically announced refusal to support and/or enforce existing laws. These laws have touched areas such as: Immigration, Illegal Drugs, and the

Defense of Marriage Act ("DOMA"). Regardless of your position on any or all of these laws, it sets a bad precedent when the individuals and agencies entrusted with the enforcement of these laws demonstrate a flagrant disinterest and disregard for enforcement. The federal government is not alone in its selective enforcement. Several States have established "Medical Marijuana" laws, which fly in the face of existing federal drug laws. Additionally, several major Cities have established themselves as havens or "sanctuaries" for illegal immigrants and thereby implicitly have endorsed the continued flow of such persons across our borders. In the shadow of unfavorable laws, many of us have chosen to flout such laws rather than actively participating in the difficult but necessary process of renegotiating the Social Contact. The continuation and strength of the Social Contract are dependent upon consensus and self-enforcement.

What message does selective enforcement send to the average citizen, who may be adversely affected or stands on opposition to one or more existing laws? Is Government in essence giving license to citizens to pick and choose the laws by which they abide? What obstacles are there to enforcement (including the disappearance of a certain self-enforcing stigma) when we criminalize so many acts that nearly everyone runs the risk of being branded a "criminal"?

The Evolution of the Social Contract -

Political debate recently has exposed the belief that, "Americans want a lot more Government than they are willing to pay for." It is not inherently wrong to negotiate with the Government to provide cradle to grave protections, but each of us must be willing to pay the price not only in dollars but also in loss of autonomy and personal freedoms. Seldom, if ever, can this be a win-win for all sides and meet all objectives simultaneously. If we as children of the Government choose to stay under the shelter of that government, then we must be willing to abide by the rules of the parent's house. This changing relationship creates an ironic dynamic: *A Government, whose source of power comes from the people, serves as caretaker of those from whom its power is derived.* It is not hard to imagine a situation where that dependence could eventually become servitude.

In the current state of our country, the negotiations regarding the Social Contract are sometimes viewed (and arguments are sometimes presented) as involving three distinct parties or groups:

- The Government that provides protection and a social "safety net" in order to assure what is deemed to be a reasonable standard of living for its citizens;
- Those who receive benefits from government institutions; and
- Those who provide the funds in order to operate the government and provide benefits.

The reality is that none of these groups are truly independent, separate, or distinct:

- The Government acts at the behest of the people. The objectives of that Government change over time, and the adopted policies inevitably benefit one group over another until some impetus forces change.
- Persons "dependent" upon the government includes everyone, admittedly to varying degrees, but the *per capita* share of all government expenditures (federal, state, and local) is approximately $19,000 per year for every man, woman, and child in the USA (or over $75,000 annually for a family of four). Few of us can complain that we are paying more than our fair share of those benefits.
- Looking at personal income taxes, more than Ninety Five Percent (> 95%) of all such taxes are paid by the top Fifty Percent (50%) of individual taxpayers, and the disparity is even greater at the higher income levels. However, persons of wealth not only reap "government benefits" common to all citizens (*e.g.* Military, Infrastructure, Law Enforcement, *etc.*), but they also benefit from the other "social contracts" among citizens. These social contracts are no less important than the better understood Social Contract that established our Government.

<u>Society as a Collection of "social contracts"</u> -

Most persons do not expect a society in which financial spoils are divided evenly. Even if such were a starting point, the realities of human frailty, as well as the inequities of trade and circumstance, would quickly result in an uneven distribution of wealth. Some may argue for adoption of the espoused Marxist mantra, "From each according to his ability, to each according to his need." However, even such idealists must accept that no one performs to the best of his abilities at all times (and as a result available resources are inevitably limited), and the concept of "need" is quite subjective (and ever expanding by all indications).

Most persons are reluctant to surrender the fruits of their labor to feed those that are deemed capable of feeding themselves. Over the years, many in the USA have strived to extend the definition of "need" beyond subsistence to include perceived entitlement to a standard of living far beyond that enjoyed by the vast majority of the world's population. Unfortunately, there has been a corresponding decrease in the concepts of self-reliance such that there is presently little shame in abject failure, and personal responsibility is all but a quaint concept. Where the potential of abilities is woefully deficient and the definition of necessaries is unreasonably broad, there will always be a tug-of-war between those who resent continued forced contribution and those who suffer from unmet expectations.

The "entitlement" mentality has extended to holders of wealth. Such persons assert that it is natural in a capitalist society to accumulate wealth and to benefit from the fruits of one's labors. However, such persons often miss two (2) significant considerations applicable to collective the social contacts among citizens. First, wealth should in fact be the "fruits" of the recipient's "labor." Resentment of the wealthy, generally comes where wealth comes without appreciable effort or where the recipient is merely a "money changer" skimming his profits from the pot without adding any real value. Second, the wealthy often give too much credence to their own efforts in "creating" their wealth. Factors, which are often overlooked but that have been significant in the growth of wealth in the USA, are the stability and efficiency of our society. These factors are not by-products of Government. Instead, they are direct benefits arising from the collective social contracts among the "governed."

While the USA has been described as a "nation of laws," our country has not been prosperous because of its collection of laws. Much to the contrary, we have been successful because of collaborative efforts among individuals that have made intense government intervention and micromanagement unnecessary. The conservative nature of regulations and the expectation of equal benefits to all are concepts generally contrary to the requisites for rapid innovation and inconsistent with the risk premium expected from investment of time and personal resources. Individuals have historically worked among themselves for a general common good. That is not to say equal results, but each person was free to seek a fair trade for his services or investment of resources, and each person determined for himself the acceptable level of risk balanced against the desired potential benefits. With greater risk, the opportunity for greater reward exists. Where the risks are real, persons will tend to act reasonably or suffer the consequences. So long as this system is seen as fair, inequalities can exist and are expected without jeopardizing the system.

Coordinating the Social Contract with Collective "social contracts" -

The primary role of Government should be to assure the fluidity and perceived fairness of economic and social systems. Governments cannot to assure that particular outcomes will be derived therefrom. Such systems do not preclude failure, but the hope is that one learns from his mistakes and with such knowledge the systems as a whole become more efficient. However, should you remove the consequences of poor decisions and the threat of failure, then risk and inefficiencies will escalate until the systems collapse. In that case, not only does the individual fail, but the systems do as well. The government's primarily role in any social or economic model should be to prevent manipulations (even by itself) that would jeopardize fluidity and perceived fairness.

Where the governed determine that any system is inherently unfair, no amount of government regulation will provide security or assure efficiencies of the system. When persons do not "buy into" the Social Contract, they willfully breach the contract, and they knowingly risk punishment for such breach because they feel that the potential benefits exceed those benefits allowed by the Social Contract. Citizens no longer feel that they are a voluntary party to the contract rather they feel that it has been imposed upon them.

Many of our collective social contracts are being breached today, and inefficiencies abound both in government and in our daily lives. If we as a collective people cannot reach an understanding on the roles of government and make a collective commitment to support and fund those new and continuing roles, government will fail us all. We cannot live our lives without risk and sacrifice, nor can the government insure us against all loss and harm. We cannot be rewarded or sustained by the government merely for being individuals and citizens. Government does not create wealth; therefore, resources of government are limited. Government can only impress wealth from its citizens. If we demand a benefit, that benefit must collectively be seen as fair, and those of us receiving that benefit must be willing to sacrifice something (money, freedom, autonomy, *etc.*) in order to receive it.

To Whom Much is Given ... *Some* is Required -

Persons of means, who have thrived by the Social Contract providing the relative safety and security of Government, have a burden and face a sacrifice as well. Hoarding wealth or multiplying that wealth to the detriment of those with whom you share social contracts will result in uncertainty and unrest. The Social Contract by which the people established Government implies adherence by all persons to the laws and social conventions that make our lives convenient, safe, and efficient.

Historically, those of means recognized a need for the labor of the masses (even if reluctantly), and the more progressive among the industrial giants realized that offering that labor force a reasonable wage and providing a reasonable standard of living assured a contented workforce and ready market for their products.

More recently, markets have extended globally, and the goals to reduce costs and increase short-term profitability by any means has meant that much production and many jobs have gone overseas to countries with a lower cost of labor.

In losing the manufacturing base, we were sold on the fiction of a "service economy," but exchanges of services do not create wealth. Ignoring *arguendo* certain increased efficiencies, if I give you an hour of my time for an hour of your time, what accretion of wealth has been seen by either of us? If persons of means increase their wealth and simultaneously remove opportunities for growth and advancement in others by investing and sending jobs overseas, then the wealthy have no one but themselves to blame when the disgruntled and frustrated masses start demanding that the Government seize and redistribute larger and larger chunks of that increasing wealth.

When wealth accumulation is seen as greed and hoarding, those less privileged will become less content to abide by the social contracts which provide the framework of our society. Crime will increase; inefficiencies will increase; and strikes or work stoppages will become more prevalent. Without timely efforts to address these problems, there could be demonstrations or riots in the streets. Such actions could undermine both our social fabric and government institutions. The safety and comfort that have given rise to prosperity could disappear.

Think about where we are today. Look at the world around us. Look how inefficiently and ineffectively many of our once venerable institutions are working. Look at the animosity that abounds in government and society. Yes, animosity and disagreement have always existed, but when you stepped back you could usually see a gradual coming together of people and ideas (even if at a glacial pace). Today, the chasm is spreading with little effort toward reconciliation.

Do we stay on the inevitable course of the *status quo,* or do we accept that our Social Contract requires renegotiation and a renewed commitment? How long do we have to wait before dire becomes catastrophic … a decade … a generation?

Enforcement of the Social Contract -

A Government that is inundated by enforcement issues cannot be efficient or effective. Not only can morality not be legislated, but the Social Contract cannot be enforced through coercion. Enforcement of Social Contract is only possible because the parties to it agree to be bound. Because the source of the authority and the source of enforcement are the same, mutuality of assent is required. "We the people" established the government. Just as "we the people" are all parties to the collective social contracts that make up our society. If the Government is seen as oppressive, the Social Contract fails. If the results of the collective social contracts between citizens are not perceived as fair, those contacts will fail as well.

Our Government can no more enforce those collective social contacts than it could vote to disband itself. The source of authority for Government and the means of application and enforcement of the collective social contacts are individuals.

Only if and when we as individuals take responsibility for our own actions, assume the obligations of providing for our own well being, and commit ourselves to actively participating in our social contracts will progress be made on the myriad of obstacles and challenges now facing all of us.

One problem is that the underlying social contracts are seldom derived face-to-face. There is no efficient mechanism to match persons with needs to persons of means. Such an interaction would conceivably result in a transfer of goods and/or services among the parties such that each would benefit. However, such a barter transaction often is deemed beneath most of us. We do not wish to be perceived as groveling for our necessaries. We do not wish to acknowledge that we are dependent on another for anything. We want to project an aura of self-reliance and control, not accepting that control under nearly all circumstances is an illusion. So, we interject the Government between the parties and say, "Take from him that which I deem necessary, and redistribute it to me for no consideration." Often, those with "needs" use the government as a modern day Robin Hood eagerly seeking redistributions of assets or benefits, which inevitably favor one group over another.

Lest you think that my observations are too one-sided or favor a particular class of citizens. I propose and acknowledge that even the wealthiest amongst us are lined up to feed at the public trough. Banks and insurance companies, which paid exorbitant salaries to the "best and brightest" minds, recently lined up to take government bailouts to protect them from collapse. Certain automobile companies were pulled from the brink of extinction by government intervention, essentially rewarding (or at least affirming) decades or mismanagement and unsustainable policies. These entities and persons failed to demonstrate "personal responsibility" and rarely received punishment or endured the true costs for their misdeeds. Some of those spared, and many of a similar ilk, have demonstrated an utter lack of penitence and unrestrained hubris in rewarding similarly unreasonable behavior in the intervening years.

Corporate America is showing recovery while the Great Recession is still being felt along the Main Streets and in the residences throughout the land. We hear arguments about the disparities between the "haves" and the "have nots." We hear how this disparity is growing and will likely continue to grow. We hear at all levels how survival is dependent upon government intervention in many different forms on nearly every level of our lives. We look to government, or at least someone other than ourselves, to fix our problems and to drag us out of this morass.

Do we honestly have faith that Government is capable of such a Herculean task? Have we devolved to the point that the personal initiative and gumption that made us an exceptional people are more memory than expectation?

The Whole is Greater than the Sum of Its Parts -

We have a lot of work to do, and that means everyone getting dirty. We must take back responsibility for personally negotiating our "social contracts." We must recognize that negotiation is a give and take. In order to reap the benefits, we must be willing give up something in return or commit to contribute something of value to the mix. We must be willing to accept the consequences of our failures. That means paying for our mistakes and thereby hopefully learning from them. Finally, we must accept that the government is not the "hammer" that can be turned to in order to fix every problem, or more importantly, accept that not every problem has a satisfactory solution. At some point, we forgot to acknowledge and accept that life is not fair, but our job in living is to make the most of the opportunities that we are given.

How many of us can honestly say that we fully have taken advantage of each opportunity afforded us? How many cannot shoulder some responsibility for whatever predicament that we may find ourselves?

The tools and opportunities exist for all of us to improve ourselves and our lives. We owe it to ourselves and our families to do just that. In order to accomplish this task, we must be willing to work cooperatively with our neighbors, colleagues, and government to make not only our needs and desires known but also to let it be known what sacrifices and contributions each of us is willing to make to achieve those ends.

A friend of mine is fond of saying, "Fix it or stop complaining about it. If you can't do one, you surely must do the other." He is much more succinct than I.

GENERATION X

Generation "X" Gets Thrust into Middle Age

J. Wesley Casteen - © 2009

Generation X'ers ("Gen-Xers"), of whom I am one, loosely include those persons born into the post-Baby Boom generation between the mid-1960's and 1980. As the oldest Baby Boomers are now eligible for Social Security, the older members of Generation X are in their early forties. Most Gen-Xers came of age in the frivolity of the 1980's. We were children of popular culture. We were weaned on M-TV and video games. We were the first generation to whom technology, in the form of electronics and computers, came as second nature.

Gen-Xers alive in the 1960's and 70's were generally too young to remember the assassinations of President Kennedy, his brother Robert Kennedy, and Martin Luther King, Jr. We were spared the horrors, at least directly, of the Vietnam War. We could not understand the disgrace of Watergate. We also could not enjoy the triumphs of the first walk on the moon, and the newfound freedoms, which were exemplified at Woodstock.

Those were the events that shaped our parents' generation. These events defined their coming of age. Baby Boomers were shaped by the prosperity following World War II. In comparison, they were spared the incalculable horrors of the Great Depression and that Second "War to End All Wars." They rebelled against what has become known as the "Greatest Generation" seemingly unappreciative that their parents' selflessness and dedication to a higher calling that made the yearned for freedoms of the Baby Boomers possible. In youth, many Baby Boomers adopted ideologies associated with "Free

Love" and by reputation at least, despised authority and convention.

As many of children of the 60's adopted the more conservative natures of wage earners and parents, they came to appreciate the efforts and accomplishments of their own parents and all who preceded them. Each generation eventually has the mantel of responsibility placed on its shoulders. Sometimes the challenge is taken up voluntarily, and other times it is thrust upon those who must act. We can debate whether those of the "Greatest Generation" undertook their great acts voluntarily or whether they were thrust in the position of defending their most basic freedoms. Regardless, the recognition is not in the reason one takes on responsibility, but in how one handles the responsibility once it is received.

In my teenage years, there was the gnawing but nebulous concept of a "Cold War," but there was no immediate threat to national security or personal safety. The concept of all out war had given way to the doctrine of "mutually assured destruction," which dissipated any palpable domestic threat. Military maneuvers took on the form of "police actions" and limited military strikes. Gen-Xers were allowed to focus their interests inward and to develop expectations consistent with near limitless capacity constrained only by imagination. We were not burdened by the realities of life. We developed a new idealism distinct from, but similar to, the flower children of the 60's.

As young adults, we fought in one of those police actions, which came to be known as Desert Storm. In those efforts, we avenged the hurt and disappointment experienced by our father's in Vietnam, and we were bolstered by the confidence and satisfaction enjoyed by our grandfather's in World War II (at least on a more modest scale).

We took this ambition and confidence (some would say selfishness and arrogance) into our working years. The structures and methods of the past were quickly falling away opening up new opportunities. With the fall of the Iron Curtain and the demise of the Soviet Union, the Cold War thawed. Technology in the form of computers and digital communications opened markets and financial opportunities around the world. We as a generation were no longer isolated. We saw the world as our oyster, and its rewards were ripe for the taking.

The resulting excesses funded the technology bubble of the 90's and the real estate bubble that burst recently to reveal the current recession. In less than two (2) decades, we twice participated in collectively amassing and losing wealth hardly imaginable by our parents and grandparents. We demonstrated excess on a level never before experienced by mankind.

This current recession comes as Gen-Xers are nearing the mid-point of their careers. We are dealing with the challenges and rewards of growing families. Our older children are themselves preparing for adulthood. Even with these responsibilities of career and family, Most of us until recently considered ourselves "young." We still maintained the perspective of youth. We sought out challenges and expected the rewards of accomplishment.

While that perspective may not be lost, it is at least expanded. It is expanded to see ourselves as adults moving into middle age. It is expanded with the realization that we are not the center of the universe. It is expanded with the understanding that our selfishness must evolve into selflessness in care for those persons and things that are truly important to us.

Admittedly, these types of realizations rarely come as eureka moments. Instead, the realization tends to grow on us over time. Many moments are identifiable, and often they are part of the collective consciousness of a generation. In the case of Gen-Xers, these events include 9-11, the Gulf Wars, and of course, our recent boom-bust economic experiences.

More recently, we have had moments, in which many of us felt thrust into middle age. These were moments in which collectively we got older. These were instances in which pieces of our youth and icons of history or popular culture were shed, and we could begin to feel ever so slightly the increasing pressures of middle age.

With the death of each icon, political figure, or hero (real or imagined), we begin to feel the pressures of our own mortality. The lives of the deceased span several generations. They may be, but are not necessarily part of Generation X, but in their passing, the proverbial torch seems closer to passing to our own generation.

Certain events are elements of the common consciousness of several generations. Unfortunately, the negative events are usually the ones that come to mind, but that is appropriate. It is not in how we live our lives in easy times that we grow and define ourselves. We achieve growth and definition of character by the manner in which we address and overcome challenges.

Through the common challenges of our generation, there is no miraculous metamorphosis. We do not awaken one day with the necessary tools and with the clarity of thought and purpose to address all of life's problems. Nevertheless, these events are guideposts for us to evaluate ourselves and to examine our lives to determine how well we are prepared for the challenges and responsibilities that face us. Where we are found lacking, we are put on notice of an opportunity to change and improve. It is also an opportunity to look back upon our lives and remember and appreciate those with whom we have shared our lives. As we inevitably move into middle age, the keys will be to hold on to some of the hope and dreams of our youth while preparing to live out our lives taking advantage of the lessons learned and the wisdom gained in living.

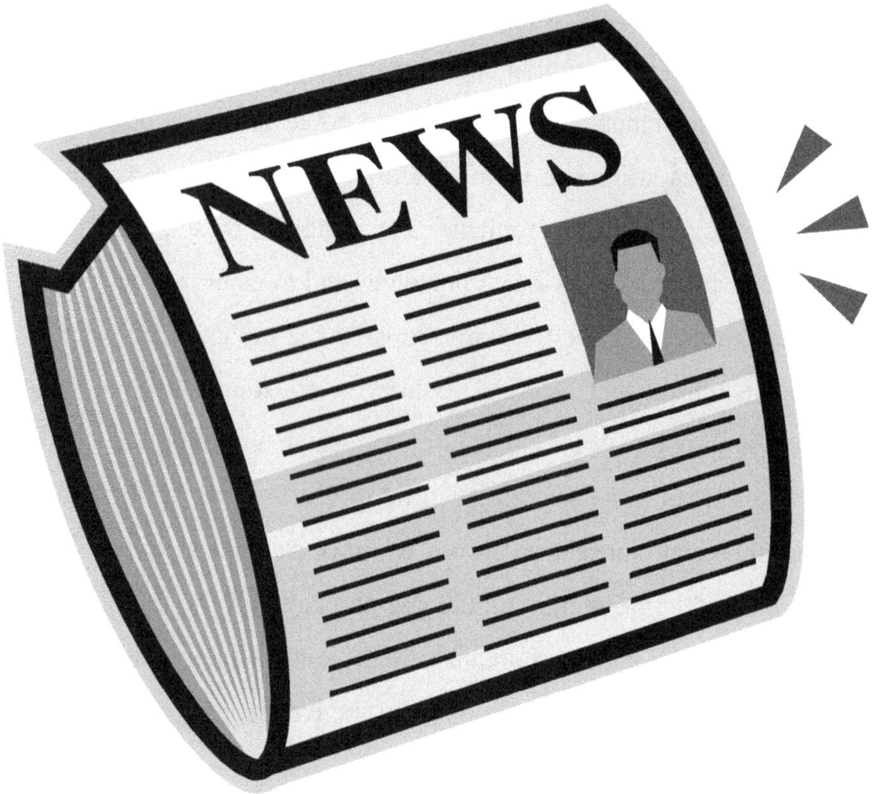
NEWS

Truth as Media Road Kill

J. Wesley Casteen – © 2011

I generally do not recommend taking life lessons from television situation comedies, particularly not ones recently broadcast, but there are occasionally notable nuggets of wisdom strategically hidden within the storylines. For nearly thirty (30) years, an episode of a sit-com has stood out in my mind as a succinct yet fitting exemplar of the proper roles of journalism and journalists.

In an episode of the 1980's sit-com, *The Facts of Life,* entitled, "Front Page," the character "Jo" (played by Nancy McKeon) runs a story in the student newspaper about her Journalism teacher, who she believes to be overbearing and hypocritical. The headline reads, "Teacher Busted in Cocaine Raid."

Since 1896, the motto appearing on the masthead of the *New York Times* has read, "All the News That's Fit to Print." As I read, listen, and view various news media today, I am confronted by what has become sensationalism in the media. Unfortunately, what passes as "fitting news" from many media outlets is often presented for its salacious impact, and the stories are often intended to arouse the most prurient interests of the audience. We have come to expect gossip, exaggeration, innuendo, and lies from tabloid journalism. Most of us know that objectivity is usually non-existent in internet blogs and the like. Often, it is difficult to discern the difference between what is intended to be "hard news" and "entertainment."

The shortcomings of tabloid journalism are not always limited to fringe media. Even "respectable" news media face unrelenting pressures to get out the story. There is a rush to be first, or at least timely, in what has become a continuous 24/7 news cycle. Sometimes lost in the rush to make the story is the search for reason and commitment to truth.

It is said that "The Pen is Mightier than the Sword," and such power can lead to hubris and corruption. Integrity in media is a requisite to having confidence in the perspective of the observer and thus the story being told. When that perspective is lost, media fails in fulfilling is primary role of informing (and yes, educating) its audience.

The line drawn by today's media in determining what is newsworthy sometimes seems to relate less to actual truth than to a cost-benefit decision as to potential damages should the story or publication been adjudicated libelous. In such instances, "truth" would not be relied upon as a defense. Instead, the media argues that it too was duped or that there was no "actual malice"[1].

Widespread distribution and perceived significance (or notoriety) is the cumulative goal of most media. Just as "sex sells," the more sensational a story or salacious the topic the more likely it is for a story to go "viral." Traditional media (*e.g.* newspapers, radio, and television) have worked to make their reporting more "sexy" in an effort to remain relevant and to

---

[1] Publication knowing it to be false or with reckless disregard to its truth – a relatively low standard traditionally reserved for truly newsworthy "public figures."

avoid obsolescence in the internet age. However, in selling "sexy" there is a fine line between that which is attractive and of interest to the beholder and that which is obscene ("having a tendency to deprave or corrupt").

The storyline from the earlier sit-com makes a full circle to explain the significance of an acronym, "F.A.C.T.," which was written on the chalkboard by the teacher earlier in the episode. The acronym was a short-hand method for evaluating a story and assuring journalistic integrity. The individual letters stood for: "Fast" – "Accurate" – "Concise" – "True."

Arguably, today's media, except in the most egregious of circumstances, succeed in applying the first three (3) of the four (4) elements. Two of the elements are met primarily out of necessity. News stories must be "fast" in order to feed the continuous news cycle. The stories are generally "concise" so as to be easily digested by a distracted and often disinterested audience. At first glance, the other two (2) elements, "accurate" and "true," may seem synonymous; however, it was the important distinction between the two that was the crux of the storyline and that illustrated the difference between gossip and journalism.

The headline was "accurate," the teacher had been arrested on suspicion of possession of cocaine. He had been arrested among several others, most of whom were guilty of the charges alleged. Using present-day criteria for publication, the rush to print the article in the student newspaper was certainly defensible: It was of interest to the reader; it would be widely circulated; and the facts were essentially accurate as stated in the story.

What was missing from the story (and which did not come to light until Jo spoke directly to the teacher after publication) was the explanation that the teacher had gone to the party to drive a friend home, that teacher did not use drugs, and that he was subsequently released by the police with the charges having been dropped. However, by that time, the "truth" of the situation was irrelevant. He had been found guilty in the court of public opinion. No explanation or retraction could undo the damage to him or restore his reputation (or his teaching position).

It is important to remember the power of media to influence the perception of what is true. It should not be enough to argue that the statement or story was technically true (or worse yet, not intentionally false). It should be the objective of journalists to assure that the perceptions and implications taken away by the audience are unadulterated and without distortion.

It is impossible to have a "F.A.C.T." without "Truth." Much of today's media would argue that the "T" is not important. They would argue that theirs is not the duty to divine cosmic "truth" but only to report what they deem "newsworthy." If media assumes as its role the regurgitation of innuendo and gossip, then that objective is fulfilled by publishing anything that is arguably defensible and likely to withstand a charge of libel. However, "Truth" should be the objective of professional journalists, regardless of whether such truths are readily apparent or whether distillation requires concerted effort and investigation. Let us hope that in the rush to make a deadline and to cash in on a story, truth is not an inevitable casualty.

II.

GOVERNMENT AND POLITICS

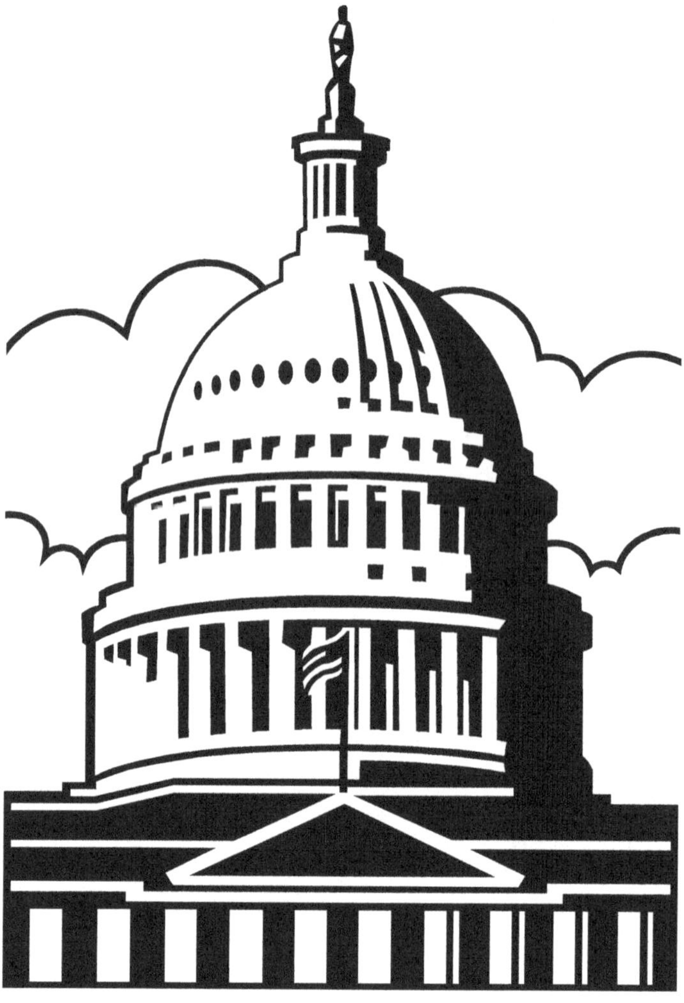

Healthcare Reform: It's as Easy as ...

J. Wesley Casteen, Esq., CPA - © 2009

<u>Where are we now?</u>

The easy answer: Healthcare costs are increasing well beyond the average rate of inflation, and these costs need to be better controlled and managed, or at least explained and understood. These latter considerations, explanation and understanding, are where all sides of the current healthcare debate fall short.

I bring to this analysis the training and skills of a Certified Public Accountant and Attorney-at-Law. I also bring my personal perspectives and shortcomings similar to any human being. I do not have a ready answer to all of the problems or some magnificent revelation that will bring forth an eureka moment. What I do have is the ability to understand and comprehend an outline or description of a plan or process that is laid out for me. To date, neither side has offered an acceptable or well-reasoned plan.

The healthcare debate has become polarized with those in support of massive changes using terms like "right, entitlement, public option, or single-payer system." Those less trusting of the government's ability to protect our "right" to high quality healthcare, and upon whose shoulders the true costs of reform likely would fall, have objected to the wholesale changes that have been proposed.

Any of us can relate stories of individuals who have had bad experiences in the provision of healthcare or who have been denied services. We can relate stories of high costs, and persons whose standards of living were impaired by those costs. We can all recognize the need to confront healthcare expenditures through cost containment and insurance, but persons who are actively involved in the discussions and debates are rarely comparing apples to apples.

Nearly everyone would agree that it is appropriate for a society to make available basic and emergency medical services for all persons who, through no fault of their own, are in need of those services and who are financially incapable of paying. The healthcare debate was originally based upon the premise that forty million Americans were without health insurance, and as a result, these persons were being denied reasonable access to healthcare.

What does it mean to be "Uninsured"?

Insurance is defined as:

*The act, system, or business of insuring . . . one's person against loss or harm arising in specified contingencies, as ... accident ... disablement, or the like, in consideration of a payment **proportionate to the risk involved**.*[2]

Therefore, traditional insurance is a means by which one pays a premium less than the potential insured loss, and the total insured losses actually incurred are proportionally divided among all persons paying premiums.

This concept is consistent with "major medical" insurance. Such insurance covers non-routine and extraordinary medical expenditures, and the insurance provides a source for payment

---

[2] Emphasis added - *Random House* Dictionary, 2009.

so as to prevent exhausting a family's assets. Historically, this is what most people thought of as "health insurance," and the cost of insurance was often paid as an employee benefit. Under such a program, the employee or insured continued to be responsible for regular and routine healthcare, including doctor visits and prescription medications.

The comprehensive health insurance product that has developed in recent years has little semblance to "insurance." It is more akin to a "prepayment plan," and the list of services and expenses for which this comprehensive insurance is expected to pay has continued to expand exponentially. Originally, programs such as "Dental Insurance" and "Eye Care Insurance" were non-existent, and even today, these programs have very little, if any, "insurance" component.

Those with comprehensive health insurance have become accustomed to negligible co-payments for doctor's visits and prescriptions. Those of us covered by such insurance have become far removed from the "buying" decision, and we have little appreciation for the "costs" of the services and products, which are provided to us. We take advantage of the services and benefits without any consideration of the underlying costs. That is not to say that there are no costs or that we do not bear those costs in the form of ever-increasing payments for health insurance.

Where we choose to be insulated from the purchase decisions and push the responsibility of negotiation and payment onto the insurance companies, we should expect that the costs of insurance coverage would continue to increase. With broader and more comprehensive coverage, we lose the benefit of proportionate risk and the resulting financial savings. We end up paying for our ever-expanding concept of healthcare on the installment plan yet we question why our premiums continue to increase.

Recently, John Mackey, CEO of Whole Foods Market, submitted an Op/Ed piece in the *Wall Street Journal*.[3] Whole Foods Market has been named among the 100 Best Places to Work in the United States by *Fortune* magazine consecutively for twelve (12) years. Mr. Mackey attempted to address several issues affecting the national healthcare system and the costs of providing medical care. He offered several suggestions based on his experience as CEO of a company, which employs over 54,000 people nationwide. One proposal included the wider adoption of High Deductible Health Insurance Plans in conjunction with individual Health Savings Accounts. (Think "major medical" insurance.) The idea is to provide a lower cost alternative to comprehensive health insurance and to provide the employee a vehicle within which to accumulate funds for paying routine medical and wellness costs. Instead of welcoming his experience and input to the existing debate, Mr. Mackey was chastised and castigated by proponents of the public option for even suggesting that there could be any solution other than a new government program implementing a single-payer system.

---

[3] "The Whole Foods Alternative to ObamaCare - Eight things we can do to improve health care without adding to the deficit." – *Wall Street Journal,* August 11, 2009.

How did we move from Personal Choice to a Moral Imperative?

The two basic issues are: (i) What is an appropriate level of healthcare for an individual or family? and (ii) How is one to pay for that healthcare? The payment options include: Self-pay, insurance, government benefits, or some combination. Traditionally, individuals have made healthcare decisions for their families and themselves based upon personal preferences, access to services, and ability to pay. Admittedly, this results in an unequal distribution of care; however, similar disparities exist in all aspects of our lives including: Food, shelter, clothing, transportation, *etc.*

The disparity in care loses significance when we acknowledge that much of the need for healthcare is entirely within the control of the patient. The vast majority of chronic illnesses are directly related to poor diet and lifestyle choices. This is not news. All of us have long known that stress contributes to hypertension, that obesity contributes to adult-onset diabetes, that inactivity leads to poor health, and that smoking causes or contributes to respiratory diseases. Despite this knowledge and repeated warnings, many of us fail to apply the knowledge to our daily lives and fail to heed the warnings. We often act in direct derogation of our own best interests. This is true despite the fact that the consequences and costs fall directly on our shoulders.

At some point, personal decisions based upon individual responsibility took on the tone of moral imperatives with the designation of "rights" and "entitlements." However, calling something a right does not relieve one of the responsibilities of providing for himself and his family. Designating something an entitlement does not assure that the resources to fund and provide that entitlement are immediately forthcoming.

What do we learn from experience?

Looking at existing government programs, analogies can be made to the proposed healthcare initiatives. The federal government currently provides healthcare services through the Veteran's Administration and at military hospitals for the benefit of service personnel. VA hospitals are rarely, if ever, held up as bastions of cutting-edge patient care, and throughout our recent military conflicts numerous shortcomings and failings have been identified relating to care of wounded soldiers in military hospitals. Do we reasonably expect that a similar government bureaucracy is going to function any more efficiently or assure higher quality services?

We are all participants in two broad-based entitlement programs: Social Security and Medicare. The financial crises, which are looming for those programs, are well documented. We hear of the "Social Security Trust Fund." Normally, a trust fund or account represents segregated and protected funds for the benefit of a particular person or group. However, there exist no such accounts or funds for the payment of Social Security and Medicare Benefits. The money paid by recipients over the years has been "borrowed" (some would say "converted") by the federal government to pay for other programs, and the "Trust Fund" is nothing more than an I.O.U. from the federal government promising to tax to the extent necessary to pay benefits.

There is an adage that, "One definition of insanity is doing the same thing over and over again but expecting a different result." I would like to believe that reasoned positive changes could be made in the provision of healthcare and the containment of costs for that care, including health insurance. However, if the objective of reform is the implementation of either a "public option" or "single-payor" system, we must consider what changes must accompany such programs.

For these options to be successful, the government, all citizens, and healthcare providers would have to change current behaviors and work collectively toward an agreed objective. The government, at all levels (federal, state, and local), would have to demonstrate a level of cooperation, management expertise, and efficiency that is foreign to such gargantuan bureaucracies. The federal government would have to demonstrate a level of fiscal restraint and financial stewardship that has heretofore never been exhibited. Insurers, medical providers, and pharmaceutical companies would have to abandon some profit objectives. Individuals likely would have to accept less choice of providers, higher demands for services, and potentially less input into their healthcare decisions. After all, "He who writes the checks makes the rules."

Even if one were confident in the ability and commitment of the existing government and current administration to adapt to the daunting responsibilities in managing healthcare, remember this is a lifelong commitment. Inevitably, there will changes in Congress and future administrations that may not have the same objectives. Should we be willing to trust healthcare to the whims of the political winds? Moreover, what if the changes fail to produce the desired results? Once something is designated a "right" or "entitlement," it is unlikely that it can ever be removed or even significantly altered or amended.

Today, we have the options of changing doctors and insurance companies. However, it is not possible to fire the federal government. Consider that nearly everyone recognizes that the current Social Security and Medicare systems are broken. Most estimates place the unfunded Social Security entitlement obligations in excess five trillion dollars. The financial fate of Medicare is equally grim. Despite these realities, it is political suicide to propose any substantive changes. Will universal healthcare coverage be yet another sacred cow, full of good intentions but lacking financial viability?

Consider these questions in light of a "public option" or "single-payer" system:

- Are we likely to be more or less conscientious if our medical costs are borne by the federal government or other taxpayers rather than ourselves?
- When determining the appropriate level of benefits, do those of us who take reasonably good care of ourselves get better benefits or less costly coverage than the moribund obese chain smoker?

- If the benefits and costs are the same, is there not some disincentive for one to maintain a healthy lifestyle and similarly little incentive for adopting a healthy lifestyle?
- What incentives are there to controlling costs and considering the true costs of a particular lifestyle, including raising a family and having multiple children?
- Do such programs encourage irresponsible behavior in which individuals have little regard for the personal and financial consequences of their actions (*e.g.* "Octo-mom")?

Is Trillion the new Billion?

Senator Everett Dirksen said, "A billion here, a billion there, and pretty soon you're talking about real money." We long ago grew calloused to federal budgets and deficits measured in billions. That word "trillion" has been bandied about in recent months with such regularity that its import has been lost or misunderstood. To put it in perspective, one billion seconds ago was just over 31.5 years. That is just more than a generation, an appreciably long but comprehensible span of time. One trillion seconds ago was more than 31,500 years. That period is longer than the entire length of recorded human history. The projected deficit spending of the United States is measured in tens of trillions of dollars.

As of September 1, 2009, the National Debt of the United States was approximately $11,740,000,000,000. Yes, that is nine zeroes, and the number is quickly approaching twelve trillion dollars. The share of this debt attributable to a family of four is over $150,000 and growing. This amount does not include the additional trillions of unfunded Social Security and Medicare obligations, and it does not include additional amounts brought about by new healthcare programs or anticipated future deficits.

Polling is all a matter of how you ask the question. Ask any person, "Should every citizen have available to him or her the highest quality of healthcare?" The answer will likely be a resounding, "Yes." Ask that same person, "Are you personally ready, willing, and able to pay more than $225,000 on behalf of you and your family, in addition to all of the taxes that you already pay, to assure that the federal government remains financially solvent in order to provide entitlement programs, including healthcare, to all persons?" Regardless of their personal and political beliefs, few will have the ability or inclination to step forward and write that check.

Congress is being pressed to pass a healthcare bill without any demonstrated ability to manage and pay for the programs being proposed. This is analogous to a parent guaranteeing his child just entering the first grade that the child will graduate with a professional degree from a top-tier private university without any consideration of the child's aptitude or work ethic, and without any thought given to or provision made for funding that education. At best, it is wishful thinking or an empty promise. At worst, it is deceitful and disingenuous.

Who will foot the bill?

Gerald Ford stated, "A government big enough to give you everything you want is strong enough to take everything that you have." Even if you believe government to be inerrantly altruistic and benevolent, it is important to understand that governments do not create wealth. Governments can only tax or impress the wealth created by its citizens. The idea being that the accumulation of these taxes can be utilized for the public good in a manner that would be impossible by an individual citizen or group of citizens.

Few of us would deny the benefit of public projects like roads, bridges, and infrastructure for utilities, or public services like military protection, and education. It is harder for most of us to appreciate and accept the use of the government's taxing authority for the purposes of wealth redistribution.

The myth of Robin Hood has been a popular one for centuries. From English folklore, we are told that Robin Hood stole from the rich and gave to the poor. His is a romantic character playing on the seeming inequities of a static feudal class structure, in which those persons of nobility and privilege benefited from the wealth and labors of the lower classes.

We can certainly empathize with persons who suffer needlessly while others hoard that which is bestowed upon them. However, ours is not a society limited by class. Each person is afforded opportunities to better himself and improve his station in life. It is incongruous for America to be seen as the land of opportunity by the rest of the world and for our own citizens to bemoan a lack of opportunity and limitations for advancement.

The current administration has openly advocated a tax on the "rich" in order to pay for its proposed healthcare initiatives. Similar proposals have been made to raise the Social Security wage cap well in excess of $100,000 in order to pay for shortfalls in Social Security. Those paying these increased taxes would not receive reciprocal increases in benefits. When government seizes one person's property, for the purpose of giving it to another, that act is something inherently "un-American."

What happened to Self-reliance?

As a society, we have developed and maintained a standard of living, which is the envy of most of the world. Collectively, our society has amassed more wealth than any other in the history of mankind. These accomplishments were not the results of bureaucratic mandates and government intervention.

America has always been known for the self-sufficiency of its citizens and the reliance on individual fortitude and initiative. Are we as a society truly prepared to throw up our hands in defeat and abandon to government bureaucracy something so intimate and personal as healthcare? Have we become so dependent on the government that we are incapable of accepting the responsibility to provide healthcare for our families and ourselves?

Hardly anyone would question the need for programs such as Medicaid, to provide medical care for the needy, and Social Security Income Supplements, to provide income assistance to the infirmed and disabled. Such programs protect and care for those incapable of caring for themselves. There is also a place for limited government welfare programs. Despite the fact that government welfare programs are sometimes cited as perpetuating a cycle of poverty among its recipients, the programs are touted as a temporary fix to allow persons the opportunity to lift themselves out of poverty. Social Security and Medicare are theoretically "self-help" programs by which a taxpayer's contributions (and those of his employer) are accumulated, saved, and returned in the form of benefit payments upon reaching an age that the recipient can no longer maintain gainful employment. None of the existing social programs are intended to provide lifetime benefits to a large segment of the population.

There used to be some stigma about being on the public dole. Respect and rewards came to those who worked hard and were committed to self-sufficiency. Today, even our most venerable public companies and financial institutions are gorging at the federal trough. Never before in the history of this country have we as a society voluntarily abandoned our self-reliance and self-sufficiency and sought to place ourselves at the mercy of the government.

Where do we go from here?

This is where I am obliged to identify certain proposals and points of discussion. I would offer that there is no one answer or one program that is going to "fix" healthcare. There is no edict that will result in universal healthcare without affecting the provision of healthcare for everyone and imposing costs for the increased services. Nevertheless, there are changes that can and should be considered to address major symptoms of a weakened system:

1. Remove the moral imperatives from the debate. There is no more a guaranteed right to a $200,000 medical procedure than there is a right that each person lives in a McMansion or drives a Ferrari.

2. Enact laws to increase the availability and portability of health insurance, and the deductibility of healthcare costs. Encourage competition among insurance companies to reduce costs and allow meaningful choices. Assure that coverage can be moved between employers or from an employer policy to individual coverage, without unnecessary restrictions and lapses. Provide reasonable coverage and conscionable restrictions on preexisting conditions. No one believes it would be appropriate to purchase automobile insurance the day after an accident. It is no more reasonable to expect an insurance company to pay for costly chemotherapy or surgery for a formerly uninsured patient, who purchased insurance after his cancer diagnosis.

3. Forget the one-size-fits-all approach to health insurance and healthcare. There always will be disparity in the availability of any commodity or service. Those that have the ability and willingness to pay are able to secure a particular product or service not generally available. Encourage the development of varied insurance products (*e.g.* high deductible health insurance) that allow persons to choose a cost effective alternative to comprehensive health insurance. Encourage personal responsibility in maintaining a healthy lifestyle and making prudent financial decisions. Assure that there are efficient programs and services available for those that are truly incapable of securing medical care or insurance for themselves.

4. Curtail healthcare costs and provide for transparency in billing. Abolish tiered billing in which insurance companies negotiate lower prices for services that are fractions of what self-pay patients are charged. Healthcare is likely the only area in which those who are least capable of paying are charged the most for the product or service. Provide mechanism for discussing and evaluating with patients costs and benefits of alternative treatments and procedures.

5. Provide for tort reform that allows fair but reasonable damage awards in medical malpractice actions. There are undoubtedly patients who are injured as a result of medical negligence and who deserve compensation. However, doctors and medical providers are not insurers of one's

health, and recovery should be allowed only where negligence truly exists. One possibility is to provide for a fixed schedule of recovery and damages similar to Worker's Compensation in cases where the showing is no greater than "mere negligence." Where there is "gross negligence" or where conduct is "reckless" or "willful and wanton" then consideration could be given to additional damages, including potentially punitive damages. This accomplishes two things: (i) Doctors and medical providers can decrease the reliance upon "defensive" medicine" in which costly tests and procedures are undertaken with limited efficacy or benefit just to preclude an argument that the highest and best services were not provided; and (ii) Doctors and medical providers would not be burdened with exorbitant insurance premiums, which are ultimately passed along as costs of services or which discourage the provision of certain services.

There are no easy answers. As individuals, we want certain things. As a society, we hope for a certain standard of living. Nevertheless, as individuals and collectively as a society we must act reasonably and prudently in determining our goals and expectations. For every goal, there is sacrifice and a price. Those willing and able to pay the price and make the sacrifices usually achieve the goal, but even then it is not assured. It seems that many persons expect to enjoy the benefits of healthcare reform without incurring the cost or sacrifice. Such expectations are unreasonable.

Tyranny of the *Status Quo:*[4]
"Defense of Marriage" in North Carolina

J. Wesley Casteen, Esq., CPA – © 2011[5]

The North Carolina Legislature has the opportunity to demonstrate the nature and quality of the leadership, which its collective members will offer to the citizens of North Carolina.[6] The Legislature is considering whether to disenfranchise by constitutional fiat all persons who identify themselves as Lesbian, Gay, Bisexual, or Transgender (LGBT). During the approaching short-session of the Legislature, both the House and the Senate are expected to take up various proposed Constitutional Amendments. Each legislative body has a version of a proposed amendment, which is euphemistically called the "Defense of Marriage" amendment, and such an amendment is touted as being necessary in order to protect the sanctity of marriage within our state.

On their faces, the respective Bills [HB 777 and SB 106] seem innocuous, and the language is likely consistent with the accepted understandings of many, if not the majority, of the State's citizens. The House Bill provides:

> *Marriage is the union of one man and one woman at one time. No other relationship shall be recognized as a valid marriage by the State.*

---

[4] Unrelated to the book of the same title, *Tyranny of the Status Quo*, Milton and Rose Friedman (1984).
[5] An edited version of his essay appeared in the Op-Ed Section of the *Star-News* – September 8, 2011.
[6] The Legislature voted to put Amendment One on the primary ballot May 8, 2012.

Most persons would likely stop inquiry after the first sentence believing the Bill to simply be a restatement of the obvious. Most would either ignore the second sentence or assume it to be superfluous. However, it is the second sentence that carries the greater import, and it is this second sentence that carries the weight and authority of government in sanctioning as a legal imperative a less than universal moral judgment and institutionalizing a belief that LGBT persons are second-class citizens.

These proposed amendments are not new. They have been introduced repeatedly in the Legislature over many successive terms. Previously, these bills never gained much traction; however, proponents are emboldened by the current makeup of the Legislature. Proponents hope that a proposed amendment will appear on the ballot on [May 8, 2012], and they hope that they can sway a majority of participating voters to embrace the perceived safety of that which is comfortable and familiar.

The fight is one to protect the *status quo*. Proponents seek to codify behavior which they deem appropriate and to smother any dissenting opinion. Such an objective fails to recognize that society is not stagnant. The fight to preserve the *status quo* is often a fight to hold back a rising tide, or worse to inadvertently remain mired in a bog of misunderstanding, misinformation, and lost opportunity.

The Legislature must decide whether to demonstrate strength, reason, and resolve in the face of unfounded fear or to resort to political pandering. Legislators will decide whether the role of government is to protect its citizens and the rights supposedly available for all to enjoy or to promote the institutionalization of bigotry and prejudice.

I am well aware of the visceral responses and connotations associated with those latter words, but the meanings denoted by them are entirely apt:

- "Bigotry" is defined as, "Stubborn and complete intolerance of any creed, belief, or opinion that differs from one's own;" and

- "Prejudice" means, "An unfavorable opinion or feeling formed beforehand or without knowledge, thought, or reason."

LGBT persons compose a minority of the population. In a strict democracy, these persons could anticipate that the will of the unaffected majority could be imposed upon them. Fortunately, our republic, inclusive of this State, is based upon principles of government, which emphasize and enshrine certain rights and protections in the furtherance of "life, liberty, and the pursuit of happiness." These rights and protections are guaranteed by our federal and state constitutions.

The rights of individuals are of paramount importance in our system of government, and any infringements on such rights are condoned only in the protection of some equal or higher state interest. The State Constitution, which may soon be subject to revision, is structured as an instrument to avoid government oppression. It is an instrument of equality, inclusion, and protection. The controlling ideals are abandoned and lost when the powers of government are flaunted so as to impose the will of the majority and limit the rights of any minority group. To the proponents of the amendment, it is not enough that there is already a law in North Carolina that contains language nearly verbatim with the proposed Constitutional Amendment.[7] The proponents wish to amend the fundamental governing document of this State to assure that those affected by that and similar laws are further denied the equal protections offered by our Constitution.

For more than a generation, a clearer understanding of interpersonal relationships and sexuality, including homosexuality, has led to the growing acceptance of LGBT persons throughout nearly all segments of society. The proponents of the amendment are well aware that the tide of public opinion and the course of history are quickly turning against them. Recent polls indicate that the majority of Americans support the legalization of Gay Marriage: Gallup – 53% (05/20/2011) and ABC/*Washington Post* – 53% (03/18/2011). The Gallup number represents a monumental shift in just fifteen (15) years from 68% unfavorable versus 27% favorable responses, and the ABC/*Washington Post* poll showed a 17% increase in those supporting gay marriage in just the last five (5) years.

As LGBT men and woman openly assume their places in society and their numerous positive contributions become recognized, stereotypes begin to dissolve. LGBT persons become known to their friends, co-workers, and neighbors as individuals rather than the descriptors "gay" or "lesbian" (or other terms much more derogatory). When accepted as individuals, it becomes evident that these persons are no threat

---
[7] N.C.G.S. § 51-1.2.

to the pillars upon which our society is founded. LGBT persons are not societal menaces deserving of isolation. Their happiness and contentment are not detriments to the happiness and contentment of others not similarly inclined.

More importantly, institutionalizing bigotry and prejudice against LGBT persons will do nothing to promote, defend, or improve upon the quality of marriages within this state. Marriage is an institution based upon a solemn vow and personal commitment between two individuals. Governments long ago realized that they could neither enforce by coercion the solemnity of that vow nor dictate the level of commitment necessary to maintain a marriage. Similarly, denying a particular committed couple the opportunity to marry serves only to ignore those things that provide happiness to those individuals and to actively oppress the pursuit of that happiness with no legitimate state interest or counterbalancing benefit to the remaining citizens.

The question that politicians should be asking themselves is not, "What is politically expedient?" Rather, they should ask, "On what side of history do I want to position myself?" Do you want to align yourselves with those who, in deference to the *status quo*, defended slavery, opposed women's suffrage, and resisted Civil Rights for racial minorities? Or, are you going to demonstrate true leadership and integrity by upholding the ideals of individual freedoms and personal rights?

A vote against the proposed amendment is not a vote against marriage; it is not a vote against religion; and it is not an indictment against those who may oppose homosexuality on moral grounds. Instead, it is a vote to uphold the ideals of equality, liberty, and freedom for which this country is known. Those who identify as LGBT will forever be a part of our culture and our society. LGBT persons cannot be marginalized for the convenience of those who are bigoted and prejudiced against them.

Those persons, who recognize marriage as a loving, caring, committed relationship between two persons, should understand that the institution is not compromised by the joining together of additional couples regardless of their sexual orientations. If the sanctity of any marriage is dependent upon that immensely personal and revered relationship being cared for as a ward of the State, the perceived attacks against which the amendment purports to defend are among the least dangerous offenses to threaten that venerable institution.

The biggest fear faced by each of us is that of the unknown. Our understanding of any issue or situation is influenced by our personal perspectives. Unless one's perspective includes knowing LGBT persons as individuals rather than painting all such persons with the broad brushes of caricature and stereotype, the resulting picture is inevitably clouded. If everyone were to take the time and make the effort to get to know LGBT persons genuinely, I am confident that preconceptions of what it means to be LGBT would disappear quickly. Unfounded fears would likely be replaced by shared understanding and an appreciation of common aspirations and goals.

LGBT persons are people like all other persons. They have the same wishes and dreams as well as the same frailties and shortcomings of all human beings. The wishes of LGBT persons that they be afforded opportunities to contribute to society, to join with someone they love, and to live their lives in the pursuit of happiness are no different than anyone else's dreams and aspirations. Other individuals do not have to understand or participate in those dreams and aspirations, regardless of whether any reluctance is based upon personal preference or moral conviction. Nevertheless, any action by the State which institutionalizes bigotry and prejudice is unconscionable and reprehensible.

It takes very little in the way of leadership to advocate that a course never change. Similarly, leadership is not embodied by following the crowd blindly hoping to reach a suitable destination. Leadership requires defining an appropriate destination, planning the route, and moving to the front of the line so that others may follow in confidence. That which is comfortable, familiar, and easy is not always right, just, and proper. History identifies turning points, at which reason was victorious over prejudice. We are approaching such a turning point. Society is moving toward broader acceptance of LGBT persons.

The destination is within sight, and arrival is all but certain. However, the question is whether our Legislature will provide the leadership to guide us to that destination and participate in planning our arrival or whether our State will detour upon a path trod by others before, a circuitous path in deference of the *status quo*. In times of change and uncertainty, we deserve true leadership. Let us hope that our Legislature is up to the task of leading by protecting and promoting the rights of all citizens.

Tyranny of the *Status Quo* – Speech Text
J. Wesley Casteen, Esq., CPA – © 2011

I would like to thank the organizers, including UNCW Pride, for the invitation to speak with you tonight at this Vigil for Equality. I am Wesley Casteen, and I am an attorney and Certified Public Account by profession. The invitation to speak this evening came following the distribution of an Op/Ed piece, which appeared recently in the Wilmington *Star-News*. That article explained my opposition to the proposed "Defense of Marriage" amendments to the North Carolina Constitution.

Rather than effectively defend the institution of marriage, the proposed amendments seek to prohibit same-sex marriage and to deny gay persons the opportunity to participate in any similar relationship. These amendments will soon be considered by the legislature, and politicians will determine whether to offer a version of the amendment for consideration by voters in the [primary] election on [May 8, 2012].

To date, North Carolina has resisted the path toward discrimination previously taken by thirty (30) other states. In adopting similar constitutional amendments, those states have chosen to disenfranchise Lesbian, Gay, Bisexual and Transgender ("LGBT") persons. North Carolina is the only Southern state that does not have such a provision in its state constitution.

In this and many other areas, North Carolina has succeeded in positioning itself apart from and above the negative perceptions historically attributed to the American South. This State has world class educational, medical, and research institutions. North Carolina has become a center of finance and banking for the nation. North Carolina also has spawned models for business incubation and development. In short, North Carolina has worked to expand economic growth and individual opportunity.

Instead of emphasizing and fostering these positive attributes and encouraging cooperation and economic development, forces within our State are working to derail decades of momentum toward equality, acceptance, and individual rights. The call to arms echoed by the proponents of the amendment includes the argument that such an amendment is necessary to protect the institution of marriage. However, the amendment does nothing to protect that venerable institution. What it does do is to institutionalize gay persons as second-class citizens. It is an effort to impose the will of an unaffected majority on an identified minority group. It is a futile attempt to resist change to the *status quo*.

Proponents ignore the fact that any tarnish on the institution of marriage is a direct result of actions by many of those who have now appointed themselves its protectors. Denying gay persons the right to marry does nothing to restore the imagined luster and shine to that treasured talisman. Nevertheless, proponents now decry homosexuality as an insidious evil capable of causing the collapse of marriage.

In their relentless defense of the *status quo*, politicians (and those who dictate their actions) ignore current realities. They fail to acknowledge that the white picket fences and picture-perfect TV lives, which were seen on *Ozzie and Harriet* and

Leave it to Beaver, never really existed. Or, to be a bit more contemporary, reality never mirrored *The Cosby Show*, on which all of life's issues could be solved in a thirty-minute time slot. Today's families live in the here and now, and to quote Bob Dylan from a bygone era, "Times they are a-changin'."

We live in a time where the majority of Americans favor same-sex marriage. We live in a time when the majority of North Carolinians oppose the amendment now the subject of debate. Many of those who favor the amendment have a view of reality that is foreign to our everyday lives. While individual opinions about same-sex marriage have been quickly progressing toward a broader acceptance, government and other institutions have been late adopters.

Those who blindly defend the *status quo* generally find themselves on the wrong side of history. Persons of similar ilk defended slavery, opposed a woman's right to vote, and resisted recognizing the Civil Rights of racial minorities. The arguments used in support of this amendment are taken directly from the playbook of those who opposed interracial marriage.

Before 1967 ... less than fifty (50) years ago, interracial marriage was punishable as a criminal felony in parts of the United States. In *Loving v. Virginia*, the United States Supreme Court in a rare unanimous decision declared that laws prohibiting interracial marriage were unconstitutional. The Supreme Court ruled that marriage is a fundamental freedom and individual right. The court further ruled that there was no legitimate state interest justifying infringement upon this personal right.

Proponents of the constitutional amendment attempt to make a distinction between restrictions based upon race versus sexual orientation. They argue that race is an immutable characteristic determined at birth, and they contend, in the face of contrary evidence, that sexual orientation is a voluntary choice, which they deem as frivolous as one's choice of clothes on a given day.

Regardless, such a distinction is moot. The argument ignores the paramount roles that individual freedom and personal choice play in our society and in our system of government. The pursuit of happiness and the right to live free of government intrusion are truly fundamental to what it means to be American. Proponents of the amendment overlook the fact that the all-important First Amendment to the Bill of Rights protects freedoms, rights, and behaviors driven almost exclusively by "choice:" Freedom of Speech, Freedom of the Press, Right of Peaceable Assembly, Right to Petition the Government, and the Right to CHOOSE one's religion.

Any efforts of the majority to infringe upon the equality and individual freedoms of any minority group are contrary to the ideals of our federal and state constitutions. Institutionalization of discrimination and impeding individual rights are proper only in furtherance of a superior state interest. There is no legitimate state interest, which can be bolstered or advanced successfully through implementation of this amendment.

This amendment undoubtedly would harm gay persons. In recent years, the significance and impact of bullying on its victims has been the subject of much commentary. Efforts have been undertaken aggressively to curtail bullying in our schools and in many other areas of our lives. By fighting to stop bullying, politicians, parents, and others have sought to remove the stigma upon those who are perceived as weaker or whose appearance or demeanor differ from accepted norms. Many persons, who identified as Lesbian, Gay, Bisexual, or Transgendered (LGBT) as children, teens, or young adults, know firsthand the emotional, and sometimes physical, scars of bullying and torment.

Can the efforts of the proponents of the "Defense of Marriage" amendments, which seek to disenfranchise gay persons, be deemed anything other than bullying? Can those same proponents expect that the institutionalization of bigotry and prejudice will do anything other than foster discrimination, discord, and acrimony against homosexuals?

Proponents wish to amend the fundamental governing document of North Carolina in order to establish as a legal imperative a less than universally accepted moral judgment. They wish to deprive gay persons of the full array of rights otherwise guaranteed to the citizens of our state and nation. They wish to establish gay persons as less than equal. However, the rights of any identified minority group should not be infringed upon for the convenience and appeasement of the unaffected majority. Such is not the "American Way."

Many of the same people, who are eager to alter our State Constitution, adamantly oppose applications and interpretations of that constitution in response to variable political winds or to suit personal whims. Those who seek to exploit bigotry and prejudice in order to protect the *status quo* are themselves threatening the nature of our constitution. They are seeking to alter a document that guarantees and protects equality, freedom, and individual rights, and they want to turn that revered document into an instrument of discrimination and oppression.

The citizens of this state do not wish to become mired in a futile defense of the *status quo*. Voters do not want to be late adopters of failed policies that discriminate, alienate, hinder, and harm. We should send a message that we are prepared to work together in order to improve our state and to make North Carolina a place where people want to live and where people enjoy life. We should work to create a place that is the envy of other states and which is a destination of individuals and businesses looking for a place to call home.

Rarely can it be argued that a single objective or outcome is in the best interests of all concerned. However, a vote against propounding this amendment is the right decision, and it is in the best interests of all North Carolinians. Should such an amendment appear on the ballot, then defeating the amendment is similarly the right decision. North Carolina must demonstrate leadership and give notice that the people of our state support equality and inclusion and that we are prepared to meet the future with open arms.

By being here tonight, you have shown that this issue is important to you. You can embody the type of leadership that North Carolina needs by contacting your local legislators and letting your opinions be known. Tomorrow, a similar vigil will take place at noon on the Halifax Mall (just outside of the Legislative Building) in Raleigh. Thursday at 5 p.m., Representative Tom Tillis, Speaker of the North Carolina House, will appear at Cape Fear Community College downtown for a "Town Hall" style meeting.

I encourage you to attend and participate in either or both of these public events. Justice, facts, and truth are on the side of equality. Responsible demonstrations of solidarity in opposition to the "Defense of Marriage" amendment will have an impact on how politicians vote. Every voice added to the chorus helps fight against discrimination, disinformation, and hate. Look for other ways to allow your voice to be heard in the coming days and months.

Thank you.

[NOTE: The foregoing is the text of a speech given at the "Vigil for Equality" at UNCW on September 12, 2011. A video of the speech is available on YouTube and can be found by searching the key words "UNCW" and "marriage" or at: http://www.youtube.com/watch?v=3e06iZQCZml.]

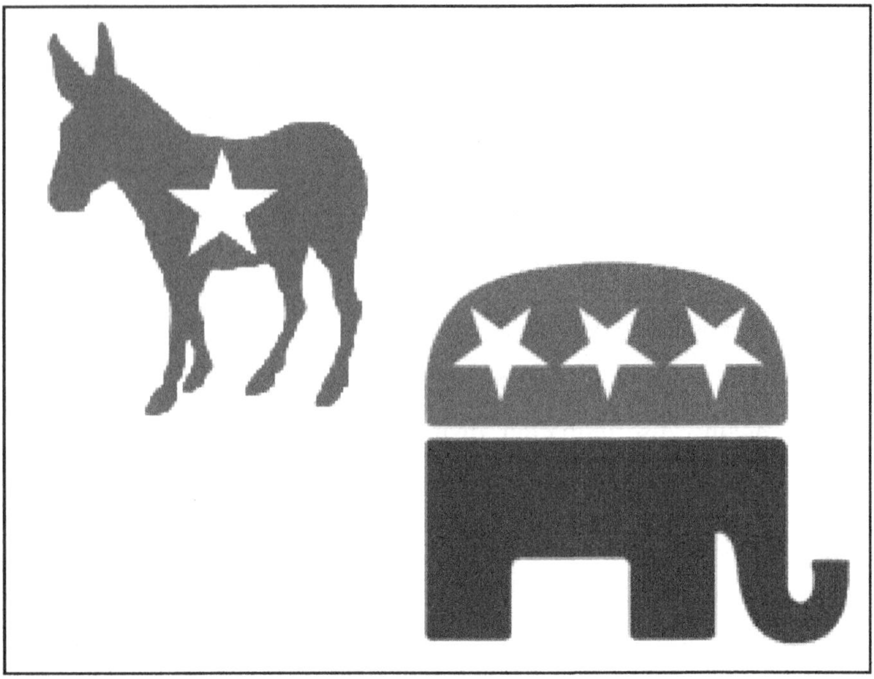

Oxymorons and the Republican Party

J. Wesley Casteen - © 2007

Dictionaries define an "oxymoron" as a combination of contradictory terms. The stated platform of the Republican Party seems to be filled with such contradictions, and within the ranks of the party you will find: The Pro-life Proponent of the Death Penalty and the Assault Rifle Owner who professes to be Tough on Crime.

However, there is a traditional foundation, which explains how all of those things could come together in the same political philosophy. That foundation is based upon the concepts of individual freedoms and personal responsibility. Nearly every traditional tenet of the Republican Party can be tied to these concepts:

- A Pro-life stance arguably promotes responsibility in the decision to engage in sex and to have children.
- Advocating the Death Penalty is intended as a deterrent to violent crime.
- Possession of firearms is a personal freedom granted by the Second Amendment of the Constitution.
- Strict Criminal Codes recognize that those who abuse freedoms or cause loss or injury to others should forfeit their freedoms.

The basic idea is that if you demonstrate personal responsibility in your actions then you should be afforded greater personal freedoms in your behavior. In contrast, if you act irresponsibly you should be required to face the consequences of your actions.

From these ideas comes the moniker: "Conservative." The argument goes that one who is conservative in his actions is more likely to be more responsible. Where the citizens are more responsible, there is less need for government oversight. A less active or intrusive government is a smaller government, and a smaller government can be fiscally conservative. This is the summary of what it is to be Republican . . . or used to be.

During the 1950's through the 1970's, there was a strong moderate movement within the Republican Party. Two of the biggest names coming out of this movement were President Dwight D. Eisenhower and Nelson Rockefeller, who was former governor of New York and Vice President under Gerald Ford. While not completely accurate, a moderate Republican can be described as socially liberal and fiscally conservative.

Beginning in the 1980's, the Republican Party made a pronounced movement to the political right. This movement is not so much related to Republican ideals as it is to a backlash from many who felt neglected or overlooked by government in the past. The Far Right has emerged as a steering force in the Republican Party. However, the agenda of the Far Right relates not to core political concepts but rather to personally held beliefs many of which are based upon fundamentalistic religious doctrine.

There seems to be a pervasive attitude of "our turn." The battle cry is heard, "It is our turn to push our agenda and to make government our tool." When using government in this way, responsible citizens, who do not support the agenda, are often unnecessarily deprived of individual freedoms.

Government grows in an effort to enforce the agenda of those in control. There can be no fiscal conservatism because money has to be redirected to promote and protect the agenda. Contrary to traditional Republican ideals, the result is "big government," or even "big brother," with a right leaning slant.

This focus of self-interest also makes the Republican Party vulnerable to the often-repeated charge that it is the party of the rich and special interests. Persons who are entrepreneurial and self-directed often find comfort in the Republican Party. They like the freedoms afforded by smaller government and the economic benefits of lower taxes. The idea being that if you are responsible enough to take care of yourself, then you should not need the government interfering with or looking out for you.

However, corporate and special interests seem to have the ear of all levels of government and the political pandering is rampant. Instead of availing themselves of the opportunity to succeed through their own efforts, these special interests have their hands out wanting to know what the government is going to do for them.

I describe myself as a Republican. Historically, I have said it with pride. I felt pride in my accomplishments, and I felt secure in the freedoms that would allow me to succeed and live my life to the fullest. More recently, I still describe myself as a Republican; however, I often append to that designation a "but." What usually follows is an explanation of how my personal and political beliefs differ from the conventional wisdom concerning what it means to be "Republican."

It can be said that no person should accept on blind faith the platform of any political party or candidate. Our political views reflect who we are as individuals, and few of us can be described with such ease and precision. However, each of us needs guiding principles and ideals, which provide the benchmarks against which to evaluate the political ideas that will likely become the legal principles by which we must live.

Ours should not be a country of extremes. Without a change of focus, the Republican Party will continue to alienate the more moderate majority. Rigid platforms should be replaced with reasoned ideals. Let us return to promoting individual freedoms and personal responsibility. After all, the protection of freedoms should be the primary objective of any government; however, without personal responsibility, no government can be successful in protecting those freedoms.

The Republican Party must revisit some of its old ideals. It is time that the party embraces the freedoms that allow and promote personal responsibility. It is time that the party quit selling its soul to special interests. It is time to focus on making government less intrusive but more responsive to all of the people who it serves.

It may be too late to save party in the short-term. Recent defeats arguably have begun the pull of the curtain on "our turn." However, political seasons change, and I look forward to being able to say the word "Republican" again without it sounding like a dirty word.

Occupy Wall Street ... the Leftist Tea Party

Blog entry by J. Wesley Casteen - October 9, 2011.

It demonstrates ignorance and hubris to believe that the problems that face this country and the world are black and white ... yes or no ... right or wrong. I have news for these "movements." Anything that you "believe" or any tool that you propose using has been tried before to varying degrees of success. You are not the first to have an idea. You will not be the last to feel that you have a mandate and have the only answer to change the world. Obviously, students of history are not common among those either in the Tea Party or Occupy Wall Street.

Government is a series of trials and errors to address an ever fluid political environment. If both sides of the debate are not willing to acknowledge the ideas of the other, are not accepting of compromise, and willing to acknowledge NOT having all of the answers, then the inevitable outcome is to stand on opposite sides of a line in the sand pointing at each other with no one doing anything to make a positive change.

Progressive "ideals" are often founded upon the Marxist maxim: "From each according to his ability and to each according to his need." The problem is that NO ONE is going to perform to the best of his ability if someone else reaps the benefits, and everyone's "needs" will continue to expand to include not only necessities but whimsical wants, as long as they believe that someone else is going to fulfill them.

As Margaret Thatcher said, "The problem with socialism is that you always run out of other people's money."

Why watch Jerry Springer when you have CSPAN?

Blog entry by J. Wesley Casteen - December 22, 2011

Those in government sometimes fail to realize that the primary benefits of living in and doing business in the U.S. are the relative safety, stability, and predictability of the society, as fostered by the government. However, when government instead fosters strife, discontent, and division, such benefits are quickly lost.

You have supposedly "serious Presidential candidates" describing the U.S. as a "banana republic."[8] The fact that such a thing can even be said without the speaker being laughed off of the proverbial stage is troubling.

If government would simply do the things that everyone agrees that it should do (e.g. education, infrastructure, public safety, etc.), do them well, and stay out of our personal lives and bedrooms, then everyone would be much better served.

Our governmental dysfunction resembles episodes of Jerry Springer, a show that was responsible for normalizing abhorrent behavior. The result being that one begins to measure "success" by not existing on the lowest evolutionary rung. As a country, we seem to have lost the desire to succeed and often fail to strive for a higher ideal. Government should lead by example not jump into the fray.

---

[8] Michelle Bachmann – "Meet the Press," NBC News, December 18, 2011.

Founding Fathers Turning in their Graves

Blog entry by J. Wesley Casteen - November 21, 2011

Our Founding Fathers distrusted the ability of the masses to govern themselves. So, they established our federal government as a representative republic. The idea was to populate the government with learned persons, who could apply knowledge and experience in establishing laws for the benefit of all. Those founding fathers would be appalled by the current state of affairs. Both parties, Democratic and Republican, have abdicated their responsibilities to govern effectively and responsibly.

The Senate has not passed a budget in nearly three (3) years. The so-called Supercommittee could not even fashion a proposal to present for a vote in Congress.[9] These uncompleted tasks represent the most fundamental function of government. If government cannot establish basic fiscal policy, all other functions will inevitably fail. DO SOMETHING EVEN IF IT'S WRONG!

The Founding Fathers feared the variable whims of an uninformed populous. The real fear should be an entire collective of politicians with conflicting self-interests. The current failure in Washington has very little to do with reasonable minds differing. Everyone in government knows that revenues must be raised AND entitlements must be curtailed. However, compromise would open politicians up to critique and criticism. Affirmative efforts would require them to justify and

---

[9] "Debt Supercommittee Members Brace for Failure" – *Washington Post*, November 20, 2011.

explain the bases for their actions and decisions. They hope that the thirty-second sound bite continues to suffice for informed debate. They would rather do nothing and stick their collective heads in the sand hoping that the masses, who they believe to be ignorant, stay that way.

As long as political choices are limited to the extreme Left or Right, any election will be a lose-lose proposition. Something has to happen to bring politics back to the center. The common ground is much more expansive than anyone cares to admit, but politicians must be willing to come to the negotiating table acknowledging that no one leaves with the entire pot. You win some, and you lose some. That is life and that should be politics. There is no shame in losing an honorable fight. Tremendous shame should be felt in the cowardice that is today's politics.

[NOTE: An edited version of this piece appeared as a Letter to the Editor – *Star-News* – November 27, 2011.]

**"Never take a hostage you're not prepared to shoot."
- Former Sen. Phil Gramm**

Blog entry by J. Wesley Casteen - July 13, 2011.

I am fiscally conservative, but somewhere along the line, the adopted banner of those who tout themselves as "true fiscal conservatives" was emblazoned with the motto, "Read my lips, no new taxes!"

Devotion to that mantra quickly has become a litmus test for anyone seeking the endorsement of the Republican Party. Similarly, the Democratic Party (with some recent exceptions) has demonstrated a devotion to maintaining without alteration a growing collection of programs deemed "entitlements," no matter how unsustainable the anticipated expenditures or unsound the existing funding mechanisms.

Being fiscally responsible means adequately funding those programs which are integral to the functions of government and to the services deemed necessary for the well being of the governed. If meeting those objectives and commitments means raising taxes on anyone and/or everyone, then so be it. If the arguments are that public safety, schools, Social Security, Medicare, etc. should be lower priorities or that these programs are overcommitted, then attack the demands and requirements of those programs directly (and offer viable alternatives and/or specific methods of modification).

Greedily holding the purse strings because your special interest is different than the other party's special interest is both disingenuous and irresponsible. Both sides are guilty of hoarding the granary stores and giving rations to those whom each party favors. Everyone involved needs to grow up.

Quit threatening to gather your toys and go home. You're playing with OUR toys and OUR money. That money is entrusted to politicians as stewards. Neither it nor we as taxpayers should be used as pawns in a game of political self-preservation and brinkmanship.

[NOTE: An edited version of this piece appeared as a Letter to the Editor – *Star-News* – July 17, 2011.]

III.

TAXATION

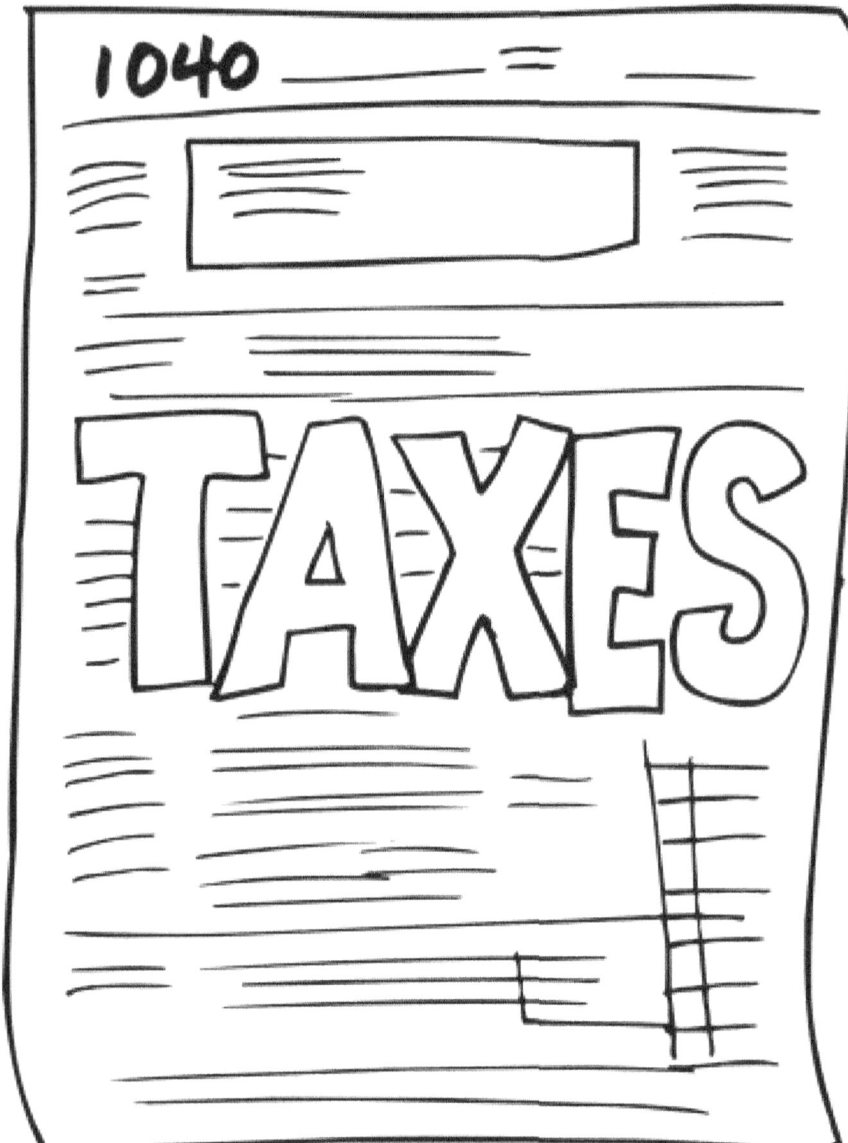
1040
TAXES

A Rose ... I mean LOOPHOLE ... by any other Name[10]

Blog entry by J. Wesley Casteen - October 7, 2011.

Numerous times recently, newspapers and other media outlets have decried the use of "loopholes" by persons of wealth and corporations in order to reduce the taxes paid to the government. These outlets are generally parroting the admonitions and characterizations of President Obama and other politicians in using this term.

However, Webster's Dictionary defines "loophole" as:

A means of escape; especially: an ambiguity or omission in the text through which the intent of a statute, contract, or obligation may be evaded.

The key word being "evaded" as opposed to "avoided." The "avoidance" of tax is entirely proper, whereas "evasion" arises from some improper conduct or wrongdoing.

What are often referred to as loopholes are actually legal deductions defined within the statues, laws, and regulations, and these provisions are being utilized by the taxpayers in the exact manner in which they were "intended." It is certainly debatable as to whether the deductions should be altered or eliminated in order to increase tax revenues; however, implying that taxpayers are unscrupulous for taking advantage of these provisions is entirely without merit.

---

[10] With apologies to William Shakespeare, author of *Romeo and Juliet*.

The jurist, Oliver Wendell Holmes, Jr., said, "Taxes are what we pay for civilized society."[11] Few persons would dispute this statement. Instead, what is disputed is the reasonable cost of that "civility" and what portions of that cost should be borne by whom.

Government cannot create wealth. It can only impress wealth from its citizens. There is a legitimate argument in favor of wealth redistribution in the United States. However, forgive my cynicism when I say that I do not believe that government is the most efficient, effective, or equitable means for determining the value of one's labors (physical and intellectual) and for fulfilling the vagaries of needs and wants among the country's 300,000,000 citizens.

I will always contend that individual initiative and personal responsibility should be the determiners of success and failure. While we may abhor those who hoard wealth, government has hardly demonstrated itself the most worthy steward of the wealth entrusted to it. Government's role should be limited to protecting economic systems and mechanisms from abuse and manipulations so as to assure fairness and fluidity. Government should never assume as its role the establishment of a defined standard of living for its citizens. Limitations of resources assure that equality of excesses is impossible to achieve; therefore, the only possible economic equality comes from reducing all persons to the lowest common denominators.

---

[11] *Compañia General de Tabacos de Filipinas* vs. *Collector of Internal Revenue*, 275 U.S. 87, 100 (1927).

Judge Learned Hand, one of the most noted and respected jurists in the history of the United States wrote in *Helvering v. Gregory*:[12]

> *Anyone may arrange his affairs so that his taxes shall be as low as possible; he is not bound to choose that pattern which best pays the treasury. There is not even a patriotic duty to increase one's taxes. Over and over again the Courts have said that there is nothing sinister in so arranging affairs as to keep taxes as low as possible. Everyone does it, rich and poor alike and all do right, for nobody owes any public duty to pay more than the law demands.*

---

[12] *Helvering v. Gregory*, 69 F.2d 809, 810-11 (2d Cir. 1934).

"Let's give the Government a little extra this year." - Jed Clampett - *Beverly Hillbillies*

Blog entry by J. Wesley Casteen - January 23, 2012.

I am reminded of a repeated bit from the *Beverly Hillbillies* in which Jed Clampett, to the consternation of his banker, offers to send the government "a little extra" this year to help them get by.

There is a train of thought that the government should dictate a minimum (and ever increasing) standard of living for its citizens, and those with means should quietly pay any amount that the government sees fit to compel. While I do not believe that wealth redistribution is a proper function of government, I would have more respect for the advocates of the position if such compulsory "tithing" were not disguised as a moral imperative equated with giving alms to the poor.

My question to wealth redistribution advocates is, "What do you think is 'right'?" ... A limitation on wealth so that no citizen can accumulate wealth beyond a maximum set by government ... if so, what's the number? Reinstitute a 95% tax bracket so that there is no incentive to earn that next dollar of income ... if not, what rate is appropriate (recognizing that, with government spending, enough is never enough)?

Karl Marx extolled the adage, "From each according to his ability, to each according to his need." The "rich" already pay taxes in excess of the proportions of both their accumulated wealth and income. Is that not already "fair"?

Government is seen by some as an idealized Robin Hood robbing the rich to give to the poor. Even an "honorable" thief is still a thief, and the rich do not have enough to give everyone everything that they seem to "need".

What do you do when there is no more to take and the contrived "need" keeps growing?

A Rich Man Moves to Town

Blog entry by J. Wesley Casteen - January 23, 2012.

Let me pose a hypothetical ...

A rich confirmed bachelor inherits land in an isolated poor community ... Tired of the hustle and bustle of city life, he liquidates all of his holdings to cash and moves to the poor town where he builds a large estate ... He holds no job, earns no income, and lives off of his accumulated wealth ...

The citizens of the town have their sustenance needs met (i.e. food, shelter, clothing, but the only doctor is several towns over); however, the townsfolk are without luxuries commonly available elsewhere (and available to the town's new resident because he has the means to import them) ...

These townsfolk are envious of the trappings of the new resident's lifestyle and feel that he flaunts his wealth ... The wealthy resident generally keeps to himself but is not abusive toward any of the other citizens ...

- Is it excusable for a poorer local resident to go upon the rich man's estate and steal assets to improve his family's station in life?
- Is it excusable for the less propertied residents to band together in the name of democracy to "tax" the rich resident and equally distribute his wealth among the residents of the town?
- If your answers to these questions differ, why so?

IV.

BUSINESS AND COMMERCE

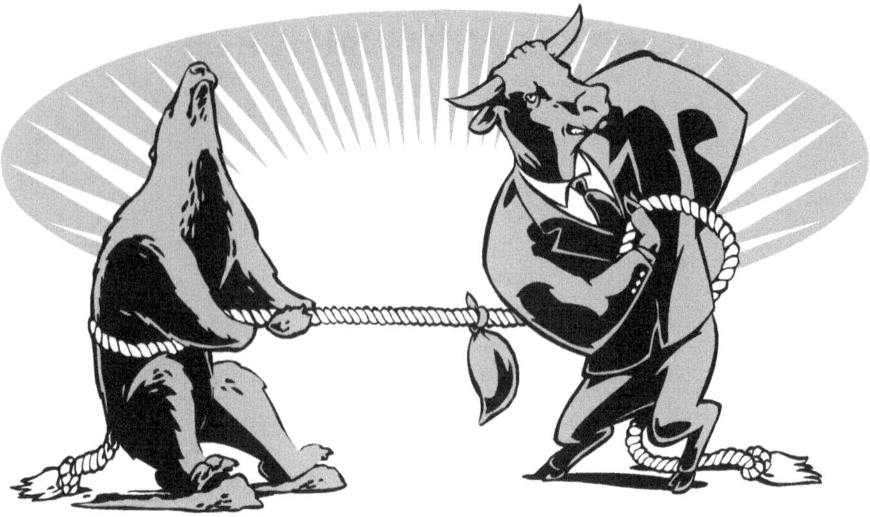

"Welcome to McDonald's® ... May I help you?"

Blog entry by J. Wesley Casteen - October 7, 2011.

The failing of a service-based economy is that it creates no wealth and barely any efficiencies or savings. Those in servitude are simply redistributing different sized pieces of the same finite pie. Eventually, I trade an hour of my time for an hour of your time. If someone has limited abilities or is lazy, he may be stuck in this scenario, but in times of economic strain, most people learn that they can do things for themselves. (How many landscapers does any one economic system really need? ... Wal-Mart has lawn mowers for $125.)

And now, the powers that be say that we are moving toward an "information economy," which may be even worse. Not only are you betting that "we" are smarter than everyone else in the world [we are not], but information is mobile and travels at the speed of light across the internet. Any good idea is immediately implemented wherever in the world the cost of production is lowest (*i.e.* NOT the U.S.). Or worse, any valuable intellectual property is almost immediately appropriated by the likes of China. (Why bother having a good idea, when you can just steal it?)

The only ways to create wealth (rather than accumulate it from the contributions of others) are to: Mine something, grow something, or manufacture something. We are already the breadbasket for the world. Mining has fallen into disfavor, and we got rid of our manufacturing economy nearly a generation ago. Look where the latter two decisions have gotten us ... $25 DVD players, $4/gal. gas and 15% effective unemployment.

You cannot (re)build an economy sending wealth overseas in ratios disproportionate to your inflows and on minimum wage jobs with the tag line, "Welcome to McDonald's® ... may I help you?"

Someone has to do the "Dirty Jobs" – Titan Cement

J. Wesley Casteen

On the Discovery Channel, Mike Rowe experiences the "Dirty Jobs" to which ordinary people commute every day. Few of us would envy the individuals who perform these jobs; however, the roles that they play are in important ones. Someone ultimately has to do the work.

Similarly, certain industries are deemed more attractive than others. Everyone likes the idea of having an IT or biotechnology company in their proverbial back yard. After all, these industries are "clean" and provide "good high-paying" technical jobs.

However, not every employer can be in one of these industries. Somewhere, someone has to manage a landfill, handle industrial waste, and yes ... produce concrete. For the persons that hold jobs with these "dirty" companies, that paycheck is no less important and no less meaningful than if they had worn a lab coat to work. These potential employees do not mind getting their hands dirty and do not mind giving a fair day's work for a living wage.

Those who oppose the Titan concrete facility have branded it an unacceptable evil before they ever hear the whole story. They oppose a use on property that is entirely consistent with the present use. The land is already used for industrial purposes, and it is home to an existing quarry and mining operation.

Is this my first choice for a new industry and employer in the area? ... Probably not. However, I am not prepared to tell anyone that would benefit from working there that his "dirty job" is any less important than mine.

[NOTE: Letter to Editor – *Star News* – February 10, 2009.]

"Old" Does Not Mean "Historic"

J. Wesley Casteen

Historic refers to what is important in history. *Historical* refers to whatever existed in the past, whether regarded as important or not.[13] This distinction is important in the debate regarding the expansion plans of the New Hanover County ABC Board.[14]

The quibble comes from those, who wish to thwart those plans. These protectors of all things historical argue that the change is out of character with the neighborhood. The most damning argument is that the razing of structures would destroy items of "historical architectural significance."

This last argument preys upon the desire in most of us that we do the "right thing." However, propounding a personal cause as some esoteric common good does not make that cause the only one, which is just and proper.

Were it not for the proposed use, hardly anyone would object to the demolition of these structures. The structures are not historic. They are old and derelict. If they had any true historic significance, someone should have stepped forward long before now to save them.

Many years ago, there was talk of demolishing Bellamy Mansion as it stood damaged by fire. There was a cry in support of saving what is truly a structure of historic and architectural significance. That was a proper use of preservation efforts.

[13] See *American Heritage Dictionary.* – 4th Ed. – 2006.
[14] "D is For Demolition: ABC Store will get Permits Thursday" – *Star-News*, July 30, 2008.

Preservation is a shield to protect items worthy of protection. It should never be a sword to prevent a landowner from making a legitimate use of its property, simply because someone else opposes that use.

[NOTE: Letter to the Editor – *Star News* – June 10, 2008.]

Beach Renourishment

J. Wesley Casteen

The *Star-News* regularly has articles concerning "beach renourishment," "sandbags," "jetties," and most recently hardened "groins." All of these articles imply that there is something "wrong" with our beaches or that they are "disappearing." Most of our local beaches are located on "Barrier Islands," which are defined as:

> *Long, relatively narrow islands running parallel to the mainland, built up by the action of waves and currents and serving to protect the [mainland] coast from erosion by surf and tidal surges.*[15]

By definition, these beaches do not "disappear" they MOVE. Historically, local beach structures were "cottages," which could be easily repaired or replaced in the event of damage or destruction. More recently, it has become a perceived "entitlement" to have a large beachfront home hugging the shoreline, and it is apparently the responsibility of all citizens and taxpayers to protect this supposed right. I have no problem with beachfront homes selling for $3,000,000.00, and more. People have the right to spend their money as they see fit. However, I do not feel that those of us not so privileged

---
[15] *American Heritage Dictionary*.

should feel obligated to shell out our hard-earned tax dollars in order to protect these homes from the inevitability-approaching ocean.

Erosion and even hurricanes are risks that these persons should have known and should assume without qualm. Apparently, it would have benefited these folks to have paid more attention in Sunday School rather than "be likened to a foolish man, which built his house upon the sand."[16]

[NOTE: Letter to the Editor – *Star-News* – June 12, 2007.]

---

[16] *Matthew* 7:26.

Big Cranes, Bigger Deal

J. Wesley Casteen, Esq., CPA

Like many local residents, I have noted with some interest and anticipation the upcoming arrival of the four (4) new cargo cranes being delivered to the State Port in Wilmington. An Op-Ed piece in the *Star-News* on February 2, 2007, noted how much of a boon this would be to the status of the port and to the local economy. While this may be true, I have yet to hear anyone speak of the ironic twist. The State of North Carolina purchased these massive cranes from a manufacturer in China. They were shipped 15,000 miles. Several recent articles and news reports have deemed this a noteworthy and amazing feat. There is one other fact that is no less noteworthy or amazing. The United States, which was instrumental in winning two World Wars based upon its industrial might, is apparently incapable of manufacturing the items in question, or at least not able to do so with economic efficiency. This puts a new appreciation on our infant like dependence upon foreign trade.

[NOTE: Letter to Editor - *Star-News* - February 12, 2007.]

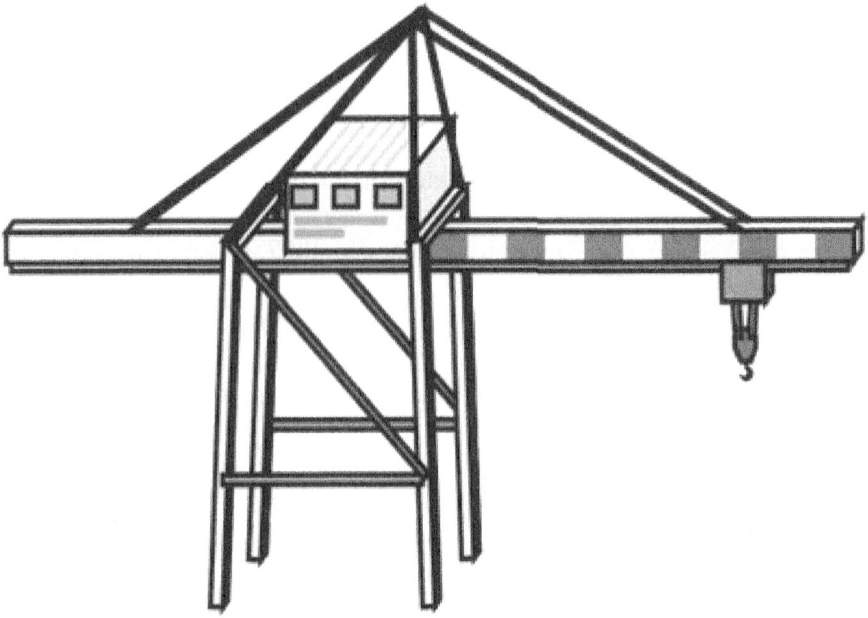

V.

RELIGION AND PHILOSOPHY

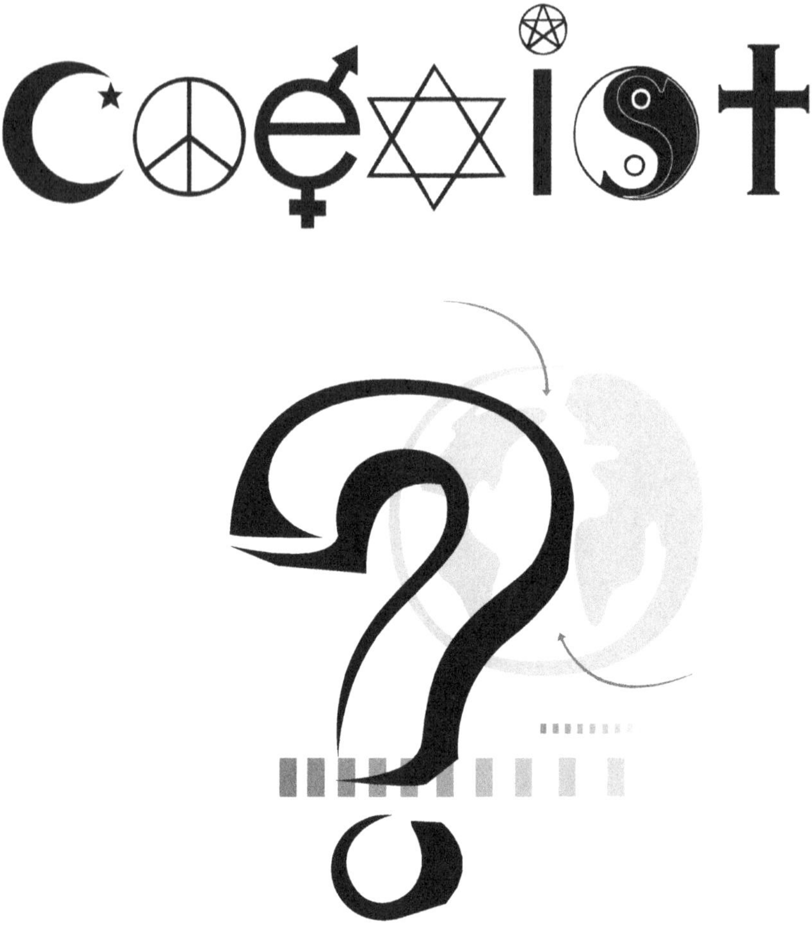
Coexist

The Bible and the Ten Exceptions

Blog entry by J. Wesley Casteen - January 16, 2012

A friend recently asserted, "There can only be one standard of morality."

Within sight distance of my residence, there are SIX (6) Protestant Christian churches (not Catholic, Jewish, Mormon, or anything so exotic). If there were, in fact, a single view of morality, then five of these churches (and all other faiths) would be superfluous, and everyone would be obliged to worship in the same church.

So, we either accept and acknowledge that moral ideals are not well defined or easily discernible, or we cast all but one of these congregations as dens of blasphemers. I am certain that each congregation would vie to be the one true church. To whom do we look to select the victor and to silence the heretics?

Reasoned men cannot even agree on the meanings and every application of the Ten Commandments, the most basic tenets of Judeo-Christian religion. That is not to say that these tenets do not have purpose, and most would agree that the Commandments (and other religious rules and moral ideals) represent points of reference to provide guidance in most situations. Nevertheless, to nearly every rule there are exceptions.

- Thou Shalt Not Kill ... unless, it is in self-defense or in support of a noble cause or worthy war.

- Thou Shalt Not Lie ... unless that lie is in support of a higher good ... such as national security or the "Church" protecting its franchise on the "truth."
- Thou Shalt Not Commit Adultery ... unless you have irreconcilable differences, which make it more desirable to marry someone else.
- Remember the Sabbath day (Seventh - Saturday) and keep it holy ... unless you are Christian and you choose to sanctify Sunday.
- Thou Shalt Not Steal ... unless you're the government doing so in the pretext of a tax.

[OK, this last one was for comic relief.]

I wrote the foregoing "exceptions" to the 10 Commandments for purposes of illustration. I wanted to show that strict interpretations of most religious laws have been abandoned by most if not all religions, except when the chosen interpretations suit the needs and objectives of the institution.

Adherents to religious dogma often question why others cannot simply adopt the same point of view or at least see things from the perspective of the faithful. However, when one or more points of view are based on religious dogma, there is often no allowance for a contrary position. In these cases, resolution of conflict between incompatible positions is not as easy as simply acknowledging a difference of opinion (*i.e.* agreeing to disagree).

The problem is particularly poignant when one uses less than universally accepted religious principles as the basis for secular laws. "Morality" laws are often unenforceable and create a chasm between the "moral," who favor such a law, and the "immoral," who choose to live their lives differently. Civility is often lost not from disagreements about the general applications of the broad underlying principles of behavior, but during the course of debates and arguments, which focus upon the propriety of relatively narrow exceptions to those principles.

Generally, we can agree on the locations of guideposts along the preferred path through life. However, we cannot ignore obstacles and detours that each of us may encounter on our individual journeys. Ultimately, each person must choose his own path, and in doing so, he assumes responsibility for his choices and the consequences of the same. None of us can dictate each step that another may take.

Unless society applies and enforces all religious rules and moral ideals without exception (which I am confident nearly no one is prepared to accept), then we must sometimes agree to disagree as to the propriety of the courses that one may choose in life. Without perspective and context, I cannot speak to the intent and heart of another. In those cases, the man is responsible only to his conscience and to his God.

After 10,000 years of human civilization, most of the easy answers are gone. In order to fine tune and take the small steps toward further reason and enlightenment, each of us must be open to new perspectives.

That is not to say that we should abandon faith and conviction, but standards of morality, just like rules of law, must be able to withstand scrutiny and reasoned debate. A man who has not questioned his faith does not understand it, and without understanding, blind faith tends to be tenuous.

Any religion or denomination can teach whatever a particular group of faithful choose to believe. However, secular laws should not be used to enforce religious beliefs where the only "harm" is an offense to the religious teaching or to the sensibilities of its followers.

Governments are established to protect the safety of the person and security of his property. One's soul and his station in the afterlife are the purview of the Church. Neither institution should interfere with the role of the other.

Some describe the absence of absolute right and wrong as chaos, and these persons equate that chaos with the advocating of anarchy. I am not advocating anarchy. The Golden Rule will always apply to one's actions and decisions. Where one sees abominable sin, another may see an opportunity to demonstrate compassion and grace.

That was the teaching of Christ when he spoke of retrieving a sheep from a pit on the Sabbath.[17] Chaos has existed since Eve ate from the "Tree of the Knowledge of Good and Evil."[18] With knowledge comes the curse of responsibility for that knowledge. The objective should be to divine truth from knowledge rather than cultivate ignorance for the sake of bliss.

This is the same "chaos" feared by the Church when it was considered blasphemy to translate the Bible into the common vernacular. It was only when "heretics" like Martin Luther

---

[17] *Matthew* 12:11.
[18] *Genesis* 2:9 and 3:6.

(German) and John Wycliffe (English) translated the Bible into the common tongues that religion advanced out of the dark ages.

I appreciate the comfort and confidence that individuals achieve in their salvation. One's decision to accept Christ is personal and unique to every individual, as it should be. I would not wish to deprive anyone of that personal relationship. My qualm arises when persons presume to determine the eternal destiny of others because those others are Catholic, Methodist, Jewish, etc. Or, more integral to day-to-day life, one decides that another who imbibes is a drunkard, that he who has sex with the person he loves is perverse, or that he who chooses to internalize his spirituality rather than broadcast it to the world is a heathen.

Evangelism is an element of Christianity; however, conversion according to the Gospel comes best from living a life that others would choose to emulate. Morality cannot be imposed by force, fiat, or coercion, and few would choose to emulate those among the religious whose lives demonstrate not love and compassion but hatred and bigotry.[19]

---

[19] For further reading about the concurrent roles of Religion and Government, I recommend John Locke's essay, "A Letter Concerning Toleration" (1689).

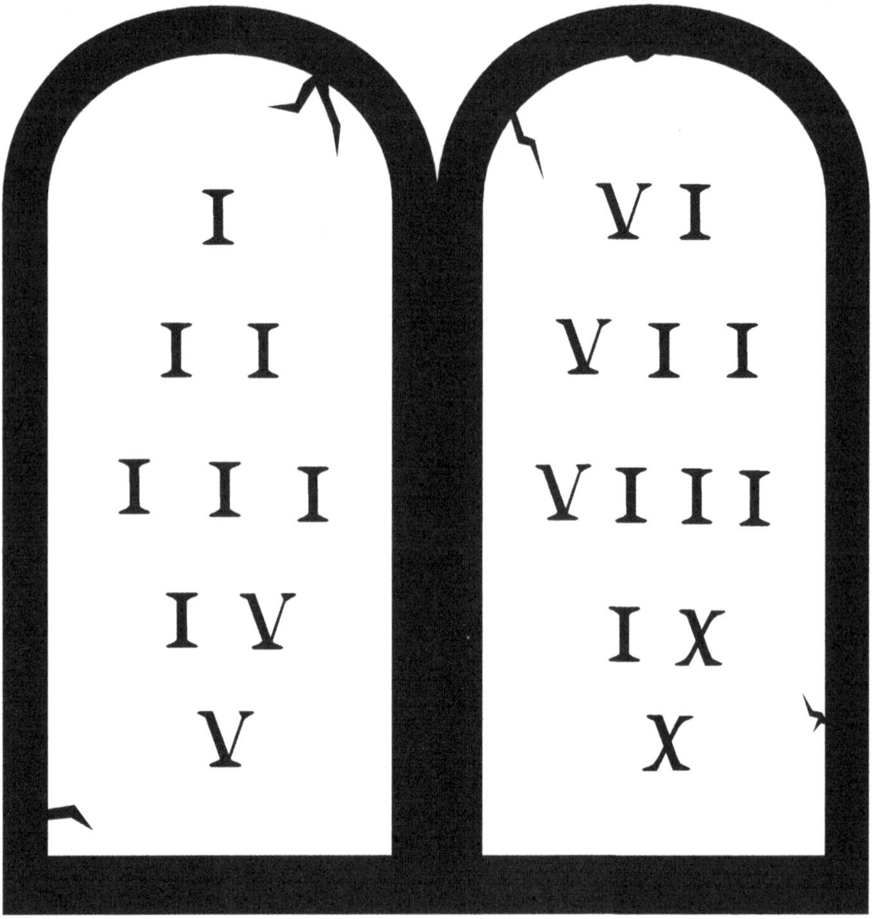
I
II
III
IV
V
VI
VII
VIII
IX
X

Individual versus Institutional Morality

Blog entry by J. Wesley Casteen - December 10, 2011.

Many persons like to think in terms of absolute right and absolute wrong ... black and white. Most people have a hard time accepting that most of life is divided into subtle shades of gray. Politicians and those in positions of authority have a hard time admitting that they DON'T have all of the "right" answers.

In politics and business, there are no cosmically right answers. There are answers that benefit more people than others. There are answers that are less traumatic than others. However, in the end, it is never a win-win situation. To borrow a concept from physics, "Every action has an equal and opposite reaction."[20] The tightrope being walked is between keeping the people happy while not putting the entire socio-economic system into an unrecoverable tailspin.

I agree that INDIVIDUALS should have a moral compass to guide them through life. However, just as with a tangible compass and map, such guidance must be tempered with grace and reason. The most direct route may be obstructed or a more accessible route may open up. And along the way, we may have

---

[20] Sir Isaac Newton's Third Law of Physics.

to stop to assist in getting the proverbial ass out of a pit, even on the Sabbath.[21]

I do not believe that INSTITUTIONS have similar moral compasses. Instead, governments and "the Church" are collectives which necessarily take on the complexion of those in positions of authority. Therefore, such institutions have and exhibit the same failings as the individuals themselves. In the end, right and wrong will be decided by each person taking to heart the admonition, "Thou shalt love thy neighbor as thyself."[22] With that put into practice, all other laws would be rendered obsolete.

---

[21] *Luke* 14:5.
[22] *Mark* 12:31.

Righteous by Whose Definition?

Blog entry by J. Wesley Casteen - January 6, 2012.

Many "enlightened" ones speak as though "morality" is a well defined and discernible point. Morality is more appropriately viewed as a range on a continuum of behaviors. Some examples of (im)morality are generally known and accepted. Laws are appropriate to curtail aspects of behavior where the identified "wrong" is (nearly) universally acknowledged.

However, laws as adopted, applied, and enforced by governments are entirely incapable of institutionalizing higher morals. Laws are rarely effective to enforce behavior beyond traditional crimes (*e.g.* stealing, murder, assault, *etc.*). Only the individual can make a decision to adopt a higher moral standard. Some individuals consciously choose standards of life short of the institutionally defined ideal.

While the self-declared righteous may chastise such "lowlifes," each person must be allowed to choose his own course in life. To the extent that one's choices directly affect no one other than himself, a person should be allowed to exist in the bliss of his "ignorance" no matter how delusional he may seem to others.

There is undoubtedly some well meaning broadly accepted religious body who would decry as "sinful" or "immoral" some element of everyday behavior, which each of us may choose as right and appropriate for ourselves. Should a particular definition of "morality," as accepted by the current majority and imposed by government fiat, have any more credence than all others?

Is there really any such thing as a "Nonsectarian Prayer"?

J. Wesley Casteen, Esq., CPA – © 2012

Increasingly, many who consider themselves Christians take offense at efforts to remove the act of prayer from public functions of government. Those who advocate such prayers see the acts as the free expressions of their (and presumably the "majority's") religious ideals. Those who oppose the same see them as infringements upon their individual rights not to have government mandated religion forced upon them.

First, one has to recognize that those most adamantly espousing the "Separation of Church and State" are often also promoting the concepts of Atheism or Humanism, which can themselves be guiding philosophies or collections of beliefs similar to any other "religion." I empathize with the frustrations of those promoting public prayer, and I do agree that the efforts to separate Church and State often amount to throwing the baby out with the bathwater. Nevertheless, the only way to insure the free expression of religion is to have a secular state. In this context the state is indifferent toward religion, but not in opposition to it.

I appreciate the irony of a secular state protecting religion; nevertheless, every governmental effort to protect the tenets of any specific religion likely infringes upon or offends some other religion. The problem arises because many religions or sects are not inclusive and tout their guiding principles as the only ones, which culminate in true salvation or enlightenment. Regardless, government cannot pick sides. It can only keep the peace.

The relationship with any deity is a personal one, and individuals should be free to vote and act upon their consciences in dealing with and implementing government affairs, while stopping short of proselytizing. In seeking to employ the powers of government in order to promote one position or to protect the *status quo*, those using such tools must realize that the same tools could be used against them should the tide of the majority shift.

Unfortunately, with the ever expanding role of government, these conflicts will likely grow rather than diminish. Nevertheless, it is good to remember that institutions have neither souls nor character. Virtues can be attributed only to the constituent individuals. If individuals do the right things, government (and other institutions) must follow by necessity; however, no amount of government power can institutionalize morality.

How [NOT] to Win Friends and Influence People[23]

Blog entry by J. Wesley Casteen - February 6, 2012.

In the United States, religious conflict generally is no more traumatic than disgruntled members of the proverbial First Baptist Church moving down the street to form the Second Baptist Church (or 3rd, or 4th, or 5th). Among Protestant denominations (we could hardly call them "sects"), the differences in religious practice and dogma are usually more cosmetic than foundational.

One would have to consider more "exotic" religions not of the traditional Protestant vein (*e.g.* Catholic, Jewish, Mormonism, *etc.*) before identifying significant historical markers for animosity and overt discrimination.

As Americans, we collectively have nearly no understanding of Islam, its principles, or its history. The parts that are known (or accepted as true) paint a picture of a collection of beliefs that do not immediately mesh with the comforts gleaned from Judeo-Christian teachings. This is especially true when the brand of Islam most familiar to us has been perverted and is far removed from less extreme Moslem teachings. Mainstream Moslem teachings are not materially dissimilar to those to which we are more accustomed.

Of most concern to me is not my personal understanding or feelings about Islam, but the repeated warnings given by persons more versed in the teachings and history of the religion and the

---

[23] With apologies to Dale Carnegie, author of *How to Win Friends and Influence People* (1936).

Middle East region that seem to go unheeded. The Middle East is not the United States; it is not European; and it is not "like us." That is not to say that we cannot coexist, but it is hubris to try to make the region "in our own image."

Instead of saying, "Shut up and listen while I tell you what to do." We should be saying, "What role, if any, do you want us to play." The failed policies of picking sides and installing governments, which are as inefficient and corrupt as their predecessors, hardly illustrate a way to make friends and influence people.

On knowing Light through Darkness

Blog entry by J. Wesley Casteen - November 26, 2011.

A friend reminded me of the philosophical argument that without Evil it would be impossible to know Good. He said:

> *Without light there is still darkness, but without darkness, light would have little consequence. If there were only light and that light cast no shadows, we would still be just as blind as if surrounded by darkness.*[24]

In absolute light there is no darkness or shadow. The light is simply all that is known. It is true that it is often the absence of something that allows that something to be defined or more importantly appreciated. Nevertheless, that does not mean that the certain something did not exist before. It only means that we are incapable of comprehending it.

The true darkness is in the ignorance of our own lives and the world that surrounds us. We must be willing to explore the darkness. We must walk among the shadows cast by fear and uncertainty. Only by discerning light from darkness, are we able to achieve enlightenment.

---

[24] Compare this situation to that described in Plato's "Allegory of the Cave."

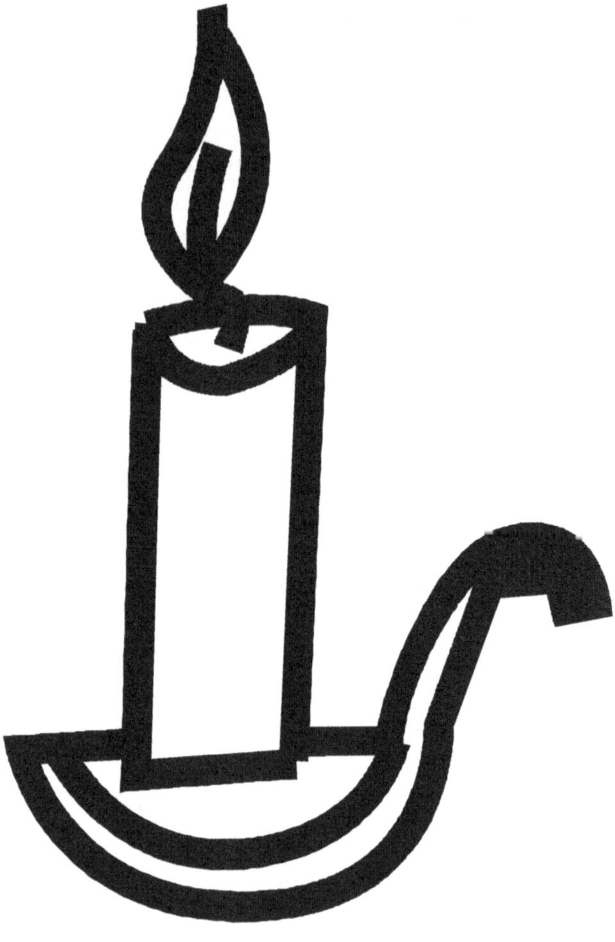

On Morality and the Law

Blog entry by J. Wesley Casteen - November 1, 2011.

One of the first things that you learn in Law School is the adage that, "Tough (close) cases make bad law." Where there are equities (and persuasive arguments about what is "right") on both sides of a case, that case likely will set bad precedent. A slight change in the facts and resulting "equities" could easily alter the outcome in favor of the other party under nearly identical circumstances.

Similarly, where governments attempt to legislate morality, based upon less than universally accepted religious ideals, the legislation will inevitably fail its objectives of imposing the adopted definition of morality and enforcing the requisite behavior on those who do not believe similarly.

If the specific moral teaching (*e.g.* abstinence, temperance, charity, *etc.*) were more broadly accepted and/or applied by individuals, then a rule or law could be easily adopted by consensus. Where large segments of society oppose an affirmative decree or where the same or similar contingents deem a prohibited behavior to be proper, prudent, acceptable, or even necessary, then the battle is not one in which resolution is well suited for legislatures. The result is that courts will likely be required to decide close cases where equities exist on both sides.

The finer points of morality are best debated among hallowed pews and divined between a man and his Maker.

Moral ideals are never enforceable by legislative fiat or secular judicial decree.

It is every person's inalienable right to live his or her life however he or she chooses (within the necessary bounds of civil society). This is true no matter how woefully misguided, ill-informed, bigoted, ignorant, short-sighted, and hypocritical that choice may seem to others. This right also extends to private organizations and to those who voluntarily choose to be associated with the same. When the views and positions of such persons or organizations are followed to their illogical conclusions, the errors of their ways eventually will become obvious to most persons (proponents and outsiders alike). Regardless, suppression and stifling of public debate can never lead to truth, nor can outlawing private personal behavior lead to morality.

VI.

LAWS AND CRIMES

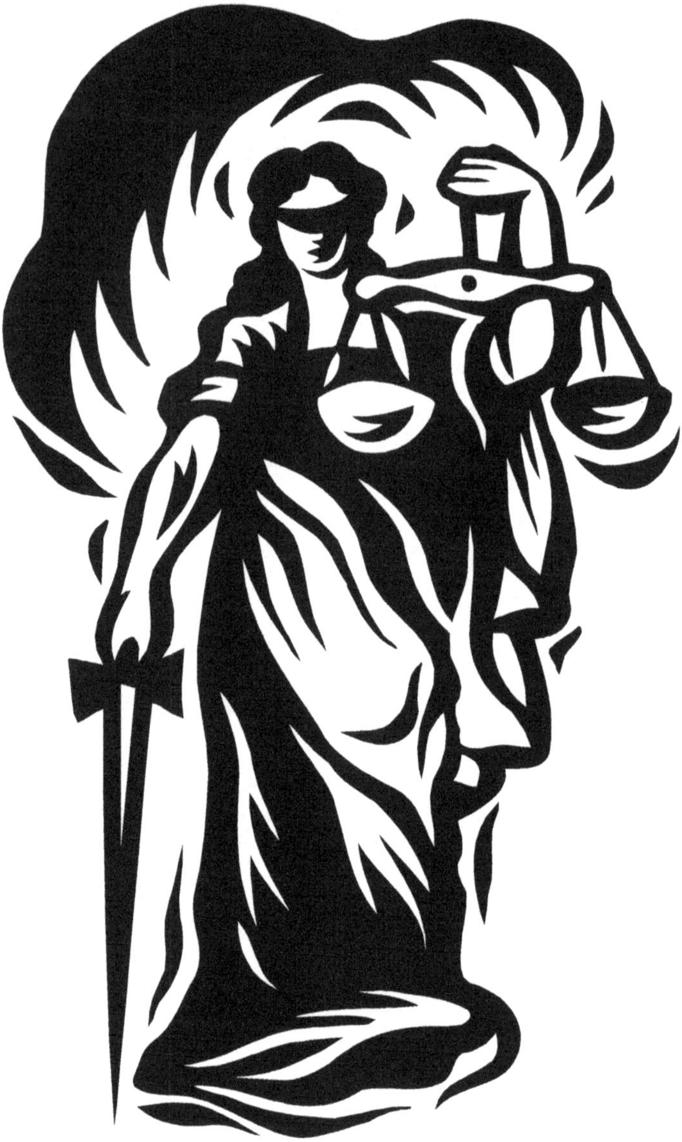

There Should Be a Law . . . Really?

J. Wesley Casteen - © - 2009

You too are a criminal. Have you sifted through your household garbage lately? The State soon may.

The North Carolina General Statutes prohibit the disposal of aluminum cans in the landfills of North Carolina.[25] Please step forward all who can safely say that they have not violated this law. I am confident that the sounds of those steps fell far short of the roar of a thundering herd.

Like many of you, it came as a surprise to me that I had been an unknowing criminal under this section. It also may surprise you to know that as of October 1, 2009 the disposal of nearly every plastic container used in your home will be similarly prohibited. However, I am not writing to discuss the efficacy of conservation or recycling. That debate will be left for another forum.

What I am concerned about is the overcriminalization of our daily lives. The State Legislature and Congress are increasingly willing to take what are moral judgments about what is good for the public welfare and impose certain affirmative acts or prohibitions upon citizens as legal imperatives with criminal penalties. This is done without the former requirements of a criminal offense that one knowingly commit a criminal act with the intent to do wrong. Instead, these acts or prohibitions are criminal simply because the laws

---

[25] N.C.G.S. §130A-309.10(f)(6).

say they are criminal. They lack the inherent elements of identifiable wrong or harm to others.

This applies to things that many may argue are prudent actions or rational constraints; however, few of us would naturally identify the act or omission as inherently wrong or expect that it should warrant criminal penalties:

- Disposing of household waste (*e.g.* aluminum cans and plastic bottles) in your garbage;
- Not wearing a seatbelt;
- Not moving over for a police or emergency vehicle stopped on the shoulder of the road;
- Not turning on headlights and windshield wipers in the rain;
- Sending text messages from a cell phone while driving;
- Smoking in a public building or restaurant; or
- Welcoming patrons to an establishment serving alcohol (*i.e.* "private club").

Again, the debate is not necessarily whether any of these things are appropriate restrictions or represent proper behavior. I wore my seatbelt long before it was a law. I have never smoked a cigarette. And, I make a reasonable effort to drive in a manner which is safe and prudent. Nevertheless, there is something distasteful about a politician making decisions about how best to live my life. I would think that there are much more important and pressing problems that warrant the attention of our elected officials.

No matter how admirable the objectives may seem, it is impossible to legislate moral behavior. Crimes represent behavior below that deemed acceptable in civilized society. Laws are ineffective in dictating behavioral ideals. Even if you agree with each and every one of the indicated acts or prohibitions, the overcriminalization of everyday activities is a very real danger to society. When minor breaches of decorum and generally accepted behavior are criminalized, nearly everyone eventually becomes a criminal. When this happens, the deterrent and stigma are lost. It is not a huge leap to the thought, "I am already a criminal, why stop at this petty crime?" Only where the prohibited act is clearly harmful to others and generally condemned as an actionable wrong by citizens, should the act be criminalized.

Many of us have knowingly violated one or more of the laws indicated above, or likely will in the future. We violate them out of ignorance, blatant disregard, or simply with the knowledge that the laws are difficult to enforce or carry nuisance penalties. Each of these reasons or justifications seriously undermines the protections of a criminal code.

When our adherence to criminal laws stems not upon our inherent sense of right and wrong but upon whether we are likely to get caught or upon the significance of the punishment imposed, we risk losing the ability to effectively enforce criminal laws at all levels. Law enforcement agencies face a dilemma. They must expend precious time, effort, and resources in the enforcement of laws amounting to civil etiquette, or accept that these laws will likely be violated with impunity. The agencies generally will choose to selectively enforce many offenses (risking unequal application of the laws) and choose to concentrate efforts on offenses deemed "serious." In fact, many laws, including the one prohibiting aluminum cans and plastic bottles in landfills, are explicitly written with the expectation that they will be disregarded.

Even where the expectation exists that the law will be enforced as written, the practical obstacles to enforcement make many such laws obsolete or nearly meaningless. This is best exemplified in North Carolina's "private club" laws. You may be surprised to know that North Carolina does not have "bars" or "pubs" as most of us would normally define those terms (*i.e.* establishments for the service of alcoholic beverages). Some time ago, North Carolina determined that "liquor by the drink" was appropriate only if served primarily in restaurants having a large proportion of revenues from food service or in "private clubs," which, as we have all heard in advertising, are "for members and their guests."

Approximately one year ago, local Wilmington officials, commanders from regional military bases, and even national media, debated the impropriety of military personnel not being allowed entry into local nightclubs. This debate raged on despite the fact that strict reading and application of the existing laws require that any person entering the club must be a member or be sponsored by a member. Additionally, membership cannot be obtained at the door and requires a waiting period of not less than three (3) days.[26] Does this sound like any of the nightclubs

---

[26] Subsequent to the writing of this article, significant changes were

or similar establishments bustling in downtown Wilmington on any given weekend?

Am I opposed to these business establishments being open? Of course, I am not. They are an accepted and vibrant part of the social scene in Wilmington. They contribute greatly to the economies of downtown and employ a tremendous number of persons. However, keeping antiquated laws on the books and criminalizing generally accepted behavior or selectively enforcing laws marginalize the effectiveness of other "more important" laws.

Citizens and law enforcement should not be put in the position of picking and choosing what laws they obey and enforce. If a law is important enough to put on the books, then it is important enough to enforce. If there is not the will to abide by or to enforce the law, then serious question should be made as to whether the law should exist.

It is likely that you are already a petty criminal:

- Do you accept this fact and risk that you may one day unknowingly violate some law with truly significant penalties?
- Do we risk losing the effect of deterrence, which is necessary to prevent actions that are truly criminal?
- Do we allow waste and inefficiencies by imposing laws that are routinely ignored and rarely enforced?
- Or, do we oppose these impositions on personal choice and attempts to legislate good behavior by demanding that

---

made to the regulations regarding private clubs as well as modes of enforcement.

those persons making our laws focus their efforts on the real dangers and problems facing us and protect the public accordingly?

[NOTE: An edited version of this essay appeared in the Op-Ed Section of the Wilmington *Star-News* – July 15, 2009.]

The Immigration Debate

J. Wesley Casteen, Esq., CPA - © 2007

Not so long ago, a caption on the front page of the Wilmington *Star-News* read, "Local Hispanics join in immigrant-rights protest." What exactly is being "protested"? I did not read anything in the article that would support a finding that legal immigrants are having their rights infringed upon. It appears that the caption should have read, "Illegal aliens rally to establish additional rights."

Let us not allow political correctness or some ill-defined "need for unskilled low-wage workers" to gloss over the objectives of the present movement. In essence, millions of persons, who knowingly entered the United States of America illegally and who flouted the laws and policies of this country, now want new laws, which afford them protections, rights, and privileges.

On the same front page, a sign was pictured which read, in both English and Spanish, "No Human Being Is Illegal." While this may be a touching sentiment, no country can safely open its borders to unlimited immigration. As much as we would like to believe in a Utopian global society, realities require that we limit immigration. For these reasons, laws are in place, which define the procedures for legal immigration.

The newspaper article identifies a lone opponent at the rally, and a picture of the sign, which she wore on her back, accompanies the article. It read, "Real Immigrants are not ILLEGAL." Immigration laws are necessary for the security of the country and for the protections of the rights, privileges and freedoms afforded to the citizens of the United States.

Immigration laws also protect U.S. citizens from unfair job and wage competition, which arises from an unregulated influx of foreign labor. The often-reported "shortage" of labor relates more to the unwillingness of companies to pay a "competitive" or even living wage to their employees than it does to an inability to fill a particular position.

I could hardly hold back the laughter when I saw Bill Gates testifying before Congress about Microsoft's woes arising from a purported need for (in this case "skilled") foreign workers. If there is a "shortage" of workers, is there any doubt that Mr. Gates' limiting future additions to his estimated Forty Billion Dollar ($40,000,000,000.00) personal fortune in order to pay a higher wage to encourage workers to go into the required fields would be an appropriate course of action?

The existing policies are no more than government-sponsored subsidies to these employers, which allow the companies to artificially maintain low wages and reap the benefits for the owners on the backs of the employees. What happened to supply and demand? When you artificially increase the supply, you remove the ability of the U.S. workers to demand higher wages. The only persons benefiting are the illegal aliens and those hiring them. There is certainly no "cost savings" being passed along to the consumers.

There are millions of persons from throughout the world that dream of coming to America and becoming citizens of this great country. Many of these persons have waded through the proper channels for years to secure that right and privilege. I have the pleasure of knowing immigrants and naturalized citizens, who have legally immigrated from North America, Europe, Asia, and the Middle East. Each of these persons recognizes that the protections, rights, and privileges of citizenship come with a cost.

For most legal immigrants, their eventual goal is citizenship. One of the last steps in becoming a naturalized citizen is the Naturalization Oath of Allegiance to the United States of America, which states:

I hereby declare, on oath, that <u>I absolutely and entirely renounce and abjure all allegiance and fidelity to any foreign prince, potentate, state or sovereignty, of whom or which I have heretofore been a subject or citizen</u>; that I will support and defend the Constitution and laws of the United States of America against all enemies, foreign and domestic; that I will bear true faith and allegiance to the same; that I will bear arms on behalf of the United States when required by the law; that I will perform noncombatant service in the armed forces of the United States when required by the law; that I will perform work of national importance under civilian direction when required by the law; and that I take this obligation freely without any mental reservation or purpose of evasion; so help me God.

I question whether those illegal immigrants demanding these new rights are prepared to "absolutely renounce and [repudiate] all allegiance and fidelity to any foreign prince, potentate, state or sovereignty." I question whether they want all of the rights, freedoms and privileges without all of the duties, obligations and responsibilities of citizenship.

Ours is a country of laws. As citizens, we are subject to those laws. Those who are here illegally have already demonstrated their disdain and lack of support for the "laws of the United States." Are they any more likely to support those laws as "guest workers"? We do not pick and choose the laws that we obey as citizens. If we do break a law, we must be prepared to accept the consequences of breaking that law even if we do not agree with it. Do we now reward those who have acted illegally by giving them protected status?

The Scarlet Letter: "F"

J. Wesley Casteen, Esq., CPA – © 2012

A series of newspaper articles have called into question whether one convicted of a felony is a proper person to hold a position within a profession or in a regulated industry. The first story arose November, 2011, when it was questioned whether an individual, who pled guilty to various felonies dating back to 1994, was a suitable person to transport human remains. In that case, the governmental authority was aware of the prior convictions and even changed its own policies to allow the individual to continue providing services.

More recently, the State Bar chose to continue the suspension of the law license of former Governor Mike Easley rather than to apply the harsher penalty of revoking his license to practice law. The State Bar's decision followed a felony plea relating to management and oversight of the Governor's reelection campaign. In Governor Easley's case he entered an Alford Plea, by which the defendant maintains innocence but acknowledges that there is sufficient evidence upon which a jury could find him guilty of the charge.

A "felony" is defined as:

A crime more serious than a misdemeanor and which is punishable by incarceration of one year or more.

In the common vernacular, felonies are usually thought of as crimes of grave character such as murder, rape, burglary and the like. The historical significance of felonies related to the fact that, under early English law, such crimes were punishable by death or mutilation and resulted in the forfeiture of the lands and goods of anyone so convicted. It is worthy of note that England abolished any distinction between misdemeanors and felonies in 1967.

The referenced news stories espoused the position that a felony conviction is a material factor in evaluating subsequent actions or activities of the "convicted felon." Persons who are convicted of serious and violent crimes are often bad persons. Their badges as felons may be well deserved, and the public may be well advised to heed any notice or warning that may be associated therewith.

However, others, who wear the Scarlet "F", are no more a danger to society than the fictitious Hester Prynne, who wore her Scarlett Letter while dutifully caring for her illegitimate daughter, Pearl. Hester Prynne was punished and shunned by the citizens of Salem, Massachusetts. In the eyes of her Puritan neighbors, Hester Prynne committed adultery and her crime was worthy of a lifetime of rebuke and ridicule. Regardless of any wrong, which Hester Prynne may have committed in the eyes of seventeenth century society, her dedication to her daughter and the example of the life that she lived gave evidence that she was more honorable and caring than her pious accusers.

Many persons convicted of felonies are far from incarnations of evil. Such persons did not consciously set out to harm or injure anyone. Given the broad expansion of statutory "crimes," particularly by the Federal Government, it is often the case that a person accepting a plea agreement and thus a felony conviction may have never known or realized that his actions were criminal.

Popular wisdom equates conviction with guilt, but the criminal justice system is not the arbiter of cosmic truths. The system is knowingly and admittedly flawed. Most persons would say that our system of justice is intentionally skewed in favor of criminals with the concept of "innocent until proven guilty," the increasingly high standard of "beyond a reasonable doubt," and the protections afforded by the Constitution. Those working in the criminal justice system accept that guilty persons will sometimes go free. Similarly, it is an unfortunate reality that innocent persons will face criminal prosecution and occasionally conviction.

There is a constant effort to maintain a teetering balance between the safety of society and the rights of individuals. The result is never perfect justice. Occasional imbalances are inevitable. The objectives of the system should be impartial justice and a commitment to learn from past mistakes and failings in developing a more efficient and effective system.

Two examples of imperfect justice stand out from my own experiences. Early in my legal career, my law partner asked me to meet with a client, who was facing a charge which could have put him in prison for the rest of his life. The prospect of an extended prison confinement was a direct result of two (2) prior felony convictions on drug charges as a young adult. We placed the odds at 2-to-1 that he would be found "not guilty" at trial, but the prospect of life in prison made even that bet unpalatable.

The client, then in his late 20's, was no longer a drug user, and he had worked hard to improve his station in life. He was far from the career felon for whom "three strikes" laws were intended. Nevertheless, he faced allegations sexual molestation of a minor child brought by a bitter ex-spouse, and we knew that such allegations never sit well with juries.

There was no substantive evidence against our client, and as confident as I was that the sun would arise in the morning, I was certain that he was innocent of the charges. My law partner had negotiated a plea with an empathetic Assistant District Attorney ("ADA"). The deal did not require pleading to a "sex offense" and would put our client in a minimum security facility for less than a year. I was being asked, as someone close in age to the defendant, to impress upon him that this was a good deal. I was being urged to convince an innocent man to go voluntarily to jail rather than face the prospect of a lifetime incarcerated on a charge, which nearly everyone believed was unfounded.

Initially, the client balked at a plea hoping that his innocence would come through to a jury; however, just as the trial was beginning, he tugged on my coattail and said that he wanted to take the deal. It was the right thing to do under the circumstances, but that did not make it any less distasteful. Some would say that the system failed him, and an innocent man went to jail. Others of us would say that an imperfect system worked as best as it could, and the parts came together to make the best of a bad situation.

Despite the constitutional guarantee of trial by jury, rarely is any person convicted by a jury of his peers. Seldom, do twelve citizens listen objectively and dispassionately at the presentation of evidence in order to determine the guilt or innocence of the accused. Plea bargaining has become integral to our criminal justice system. The vast majority of criminal defendants choose to plea to fewer charges or less serious crimes than those originally charged rather than risk the uncertainty of a trial. Some analyses indicate greater than ninety percent (90%) of criminal cases are decided in this manner. The government (prosecutors and judges) participate in plea bargaining for the sake of judicial economy and efficiency, recognizing that trials by jury on all criminal charges are impracticable. Trying each and every case, for which trial by jury is allowed, would bring the criminal justice system to a screeching halt.

Many would argue that there are abuses on both sides. The system can be abused by guilty persons, who know that they are unlikely to face the maximum punishment possible for their crimes, and they become repeat offenders. Similarly, the government can abuse the system by tacking on numerous charges to increase the potential punishment faced by a defendant in a marginal or questionable case, with the objective being to encourage (some would say "coerce") that defendant to plead to a reduced charge simply to assure a "conviction."

Idealists may question why any defendant would plead to a charge for which he believes and maintains his innocence. Like my example above, the potential prison time faced by such a defendant may be measured in decades. Depending on the defendant's age, it may effectively be a life sentence. Sentencing guidelines, all but assure that a defendant found guilty at trial will receive the maximum possible sentence. Whereas, a negotiated plea, even on a felony charge, may result in a minimal prison stay or even probation. Additionally, the cost of a trial can be tens of thousands up to hundreds of thousands of dollars, depending on the complexity of the case. The costs of defense and trial can easily bankrupt a defendant and his family. Even court-appointed attorneys are not free, unless the defendant is found "not guilty."

Some time ago, I attended an administrative hearing in which a former professional licensee was seeking reinstatement of his licensee in a forum similar to the one recently utilized by former Governor Mike Easley relating to his law license. The former licensee had pled to and been punished for a felony conviction under federal law. Unlike the State Bar in considering the status of Governor Easley, the licensing board in question historically has taken the position that any felony conviction was sufficient cause in and of itself to revoke the licensee's privilege to practice his chosen profession. Initially, there had been little or no consideration given as to how, or if at all, the actions giving rise to the felony impeded the licensee's ability to practice.

I attended the hearing with a colleague, who had formerly sat on the national board charged with determining the rules and procedures which the licensee had been accused of violating. That colleague, coincidentally, had testified on behalf of the licensee at the original revocation hearing. She had testified that there had been technical errors or omissions, but that these errors were at most inadvertent simple negligence. There was no indication of willfulness, gross negligence, or reckless behavior, much less a knowing wrong or actual intent to harm on the part of the licensee.

It was interesting to hear the tenor of the debate and watch the responses of the members of the licensing board. For some, the issue was black and white, "He was convicted of a felony; therefore, he is unworthy to ever again be licensed in the profession." Others realized, "There but for the grace of God go I." The latter contingent was more inclined to consider the person as a whole rather than focus on an isolated act or incident (or his status as a "convicted felon").

In the discussions that followed, the nature of the error was discussed, but more interesting was the explanation of how the licensee came to plead to the felony. He had been caught in the wide net of a series of federal criminal statutes known as "honest services laws." Using these provisions, federal prosecutors often sought criminal convictions based upon fraud committed by denying someone the "intangible right" to one's "honest services." Under applications by some courts, no intent to do harm was required. All that had to be shown was an act or omission outside a prescribed standard of care. Additionally, each party allegedly harmed could represent an additional count or charge arising from the same isolated act or series of related actions.[27]

The licensee in question faced multiple counts, and convictions on all counts would have resulted in decades in a

---

[27] The U.S. Supreme Court greatly curtailed the use of these laws after 2009.

federal prison. Given the technical complexities and number of counts, defense against the charges was entirely cost prohibitive. In the end, he opted to plead to one felony and received probation with no active prison time. He did this to save himself and his family the trauma of a protracted trial and financial ruin. Only the most adamant among us would argue that he would have refused a plea under the circumstances.

By any measure, the individual paid his debt to society. A series of witnesses attested to his technical competence, work ethic, and personal character. Nevertheless, the hearing focused on whether one convicted of a felony ever could be qualified thereafter to practice as a member of a regulated profession. The recent consideration given by the State Bar to Governor Easley would tend to hold open that possibility. For others, the thought is, "Once and always a felon."

As to the recent newspaper stories, I do not know the specific facts or details beyond what has been reported publically. I do not know the circumstances of the pleas. I do not know personally the individuals involved, and I am not qualified to make a judgment based upon those limited facts as to whether these persons are suited to perform the duties of their jobs or worthy of the confidence and franchise of the agencies charged with regulating their professions. Nevertheless, I am willing to allow those government agencies to do the jobs with which they are tasked and to trust those bodies to fulfill their obligations to protect the public interests. I am unwilling to forever brand an entire class of persons as outcasts based solely upon their status as felons and without consideration of them as individuals. None of us would want such a fate for ourselves.

Persons stereotype others because it makes interactions with those in the stereotyped group or class easy and predictable. It is much easier to paint with a broad brush than with a fine one. Society assumes that a felon is a bad person. This assumption may often prove true. However, not everyone fits the expected mold. People do not always adhere to the script that we write for them. We may take comfort in separating ourselves from felons, but a great harm comes from taking the next step in assuming that we are better than anyone who was convicted of a felony or that, as an individual, a convicted felon may not have something beneficial to contribute to society.

The collective experiences of society and we as individuals may support what we believe to be the personality and character traits of convicted felons. Undoubtedly, there are people who are convicted of dangerous crimes and whose convictions properly serve as warnings for all to approach them with care. However, blanket assumptions seldom, if ever, apply to everyone in a given group or class. Perhaps, it is appropriate to decide that a convicted felon can never be rehabilitated sufficiently to perform certain jobs and duties. However, we should make that decision informed of all of the facts and circumstances, and we should ask ourselves whether the Scarlet Letter that they wear truly serves to protect society.[28]

---

[28] An edited version of this essay was published in the Op-Ed Section of *North Carolina Lawyers Weekly* – February 13, 2012.

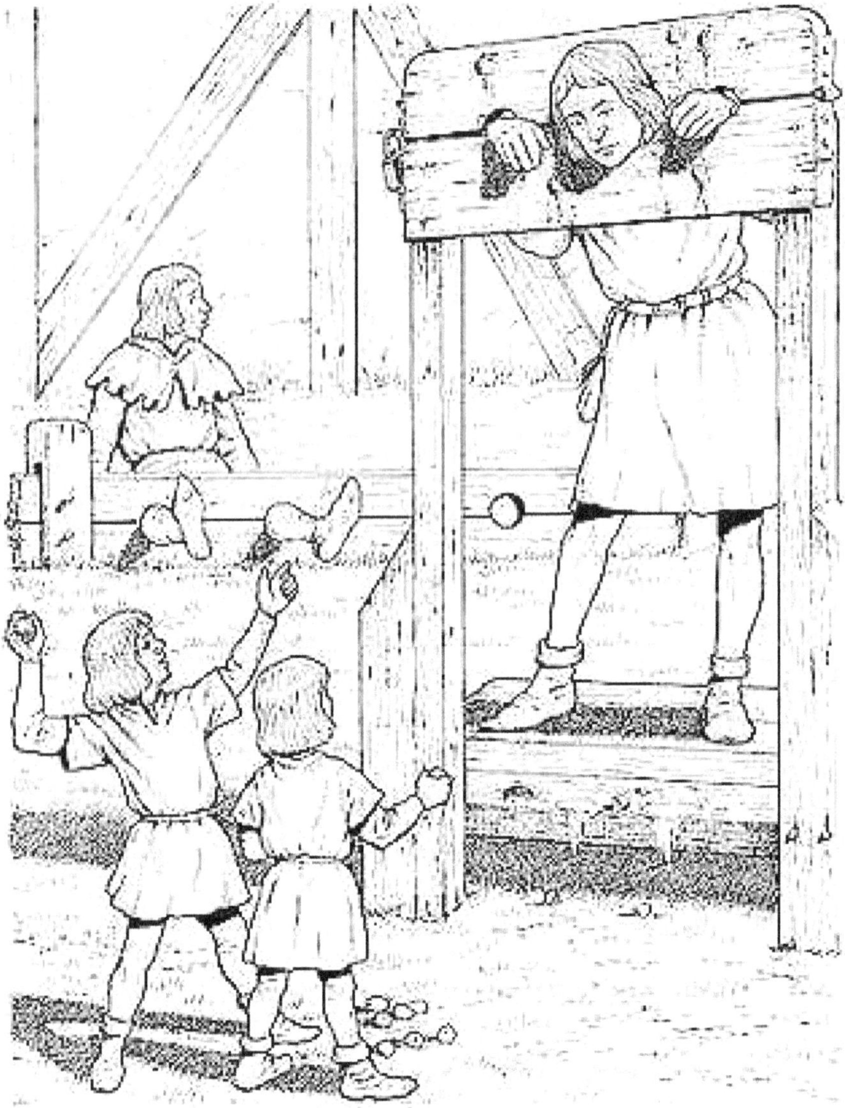

VII.

MISCELLANEOUS

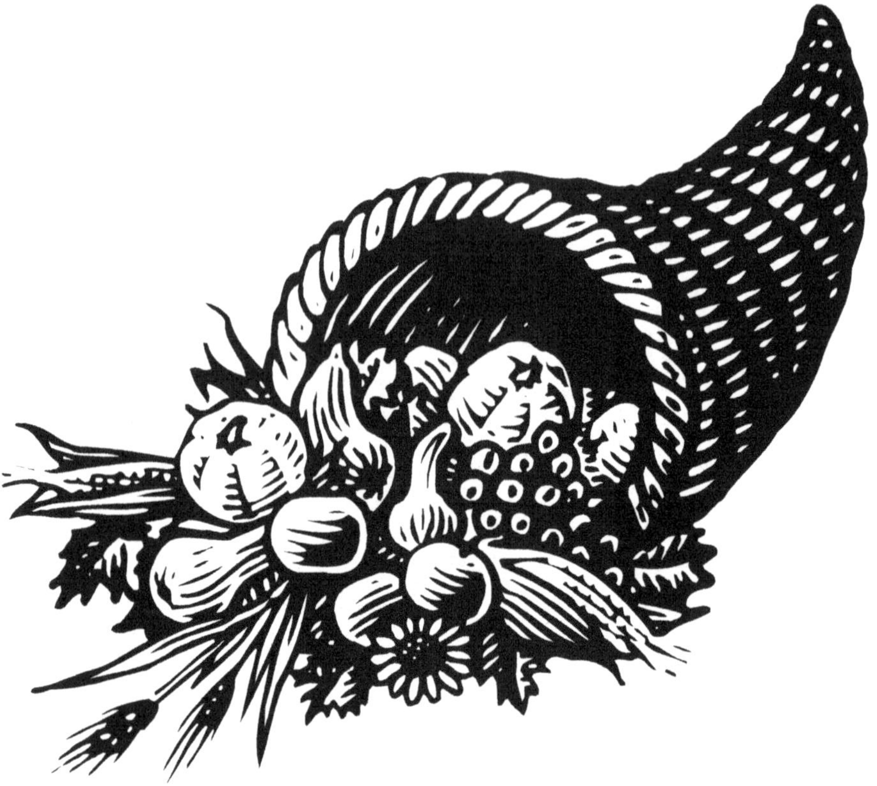

Happiness versus the Pursuit Thereof

Blog entry by J. Wesley Casteen - August 8, 2011.

OBSERVATION #1: The guarantee allowing the "pursuit of happiness" does not require that everyone achieve his or her own self-defined level of happiness. (Not everyone can be one of those much maligned "millionaires.")

OBSERVATION #2: "Equality" will never be achieved by raising everyone to some Utopian standard of living. The only achievable equality is devolution of society to the lowest common denominator. Risk and investment of time and resources require the opportunity for a premium to be paid on that investment.

OBSERVATION #3: "From each according to his abilities ... to each according to his needs" runs contrary to human nature. Most persons are by nature lazy and selfish. One with abilities is not likely to perform to the best of those abilities (thereby filling the government stores) if the benefits are given to others. Similarly, one whose needs are fulfilled by the government is unlikely to contribute to filling his own needs. A man who has no fear of starvation has no incentive to feed himself.

OBSERVATION #4: Life is not fair. It never has been and never will be. There will always be poor people. There will always be people that succumb to their own personal failings, limitations, or shortcomings. A life well lived should not be measured in absolutes, but against whether we make the most of the opportunities that each of us is given.

"The Ten Cannots" by the Rev. William Boetcker (1916)

Posted by Wesley Casteen on Tuesday, January 31, 2012.

Rules by which to Live ...

1. *You cannot bring about prosperity by discouraging thrift.*

2. *You cannot strengthen the weak by weakening the strong.*

3. *You cannot help small men by tearing down big men.*

4. *You cannot help the poor by destroying the rich.*

5. *You cannot lift the wage-earner by pulling down the wage-payer.*

6. *You cannot keep out of trouble by spending more than your income.*

7. *You cannot further the brotherhood of man by inciting class hatred.*

8. *You cannot establish sound security on borrowed money.*

9. *You cannot build character and courage by taking away a man's initiative and independence.*

10. *You cannot help men permanently by doing for them what they can and should do for themselves.*

The statements above are regularly – and falsely – attributed to Abraham Lincoln, according to Lincoln expert and Illinois State Historian Thomas F. Schwartz in an article posted on the Illinois Historic Preservation Agency's website. The quotes are the work of Boetcker, a Presbyterian minister and conservative political activist who published them as "The Ten Cannots" in 1916.

Melvin v. Easley, 7 Jones (NC) 356, 52 NC 356, (1860)

Posted by J. Wesley Casteen - October 7, 2011.

... The leading idea in the original framework of our government, and in the subsequent legislative and executive action under it, has been to leave men as free as is consistent with safety -- to interfere no more with social liberty, by law, than is needful to secure order and the rights of each and every one. Outside of this, it is left to the individual citizen to govern himself -- guided by the religious and moral teachings to which he is accustomed to resort, and hence the spirit of individual responsibility, of independence and self-reliance, which is so remarkably characteristic of the American people, and which has given such force and effect to our institutions. Of all the classes of human rights, those which belong to conscience, in the worship of God, are held the most sacred. They cannot be touched without arousing public attention and censure, and it is the last subject on which the State would resort to legislation, not actually needed for political safety and repose [peace]. ...

THE END

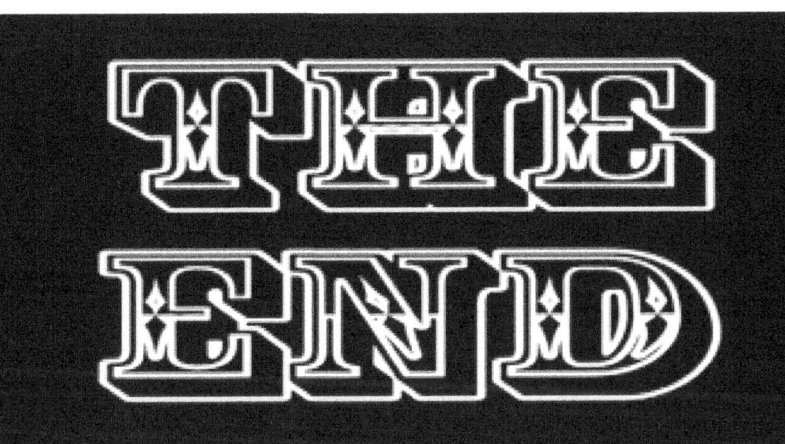

ABOUT THE AUTHOR: *www.casteen.org*

J. Wesley Casteen was born in Fort Riley, Kansas just prior to his father and namesake mustering out of the United States Army. He moved with his parents back to their hometown in eastern North Carolina where he was reared along with a younger brother.

Wesley graduated from James Kenan High School in Warsaw, North Carolina, and attended college at Wake Forest University, where he received his undergraduate degree (B.S.) in Accounting. He passed the Certified Public Accountant (CPA) examination and worked in public accounting before returning to Law School.

He graduated *cum laude* with a *Juris Doctor* (J.D.) degree from the Norman A. Wiggins School of law at Campbell University, and he has practiced law throughout the state of North Carolina. Wesley recently received an advanced academic law degree (LL.M.) with a concentration in Taxation from the University of Alabama, where he also graduated *cum laude*.

Wesley speaks regularly at continuing education seminars for both attorneys and CPA's, and his writings have been published in several professional publications and newspapers. He has received specialty designations from the American Institute of Certified Public Accountants (AICPA), including being Accredited in Business Valuations (ABV) and Certified in Financial Forensics (CFF).

Wesley presently lives and practices law in Wilmington, North Carolina, and his practice is concentrated in the areas of: Business Law, Commercial Transactions, Estate Planning, Taxation, and Civil Litigation.

Wesley has been active in numerous civic and professional organizations, and he has held positions with committees of the North Carolina State Bar, as well as leadership positions with the Tenth (10th) District Bar, where he was President in 2009, and the North Carolina Association of CPA's (NCACPA), where he presently serves on the association's Board of Directors.

Made in the USA
Columbia, SC
11 November 2022